# THE
# DAY
# THE
# LOVING
# STOPPED

# THE DAY THE LOVING STOPPED

## A Daughter's View of Her Parents' Divorce

## *Julie Autumn List*

**Seaview Books**
NEW YORK

Library of Congress Cataloging in Publication Data

List, Julie Autumn.
    The day the loving stopped.

    1. List, Julie Autumn. 2. Children of divorced parents—Biography. I. Title.
HQ777.5.L57      301.42'84'0924      79-66075
ISBN 0-87223-559-9

This book is for:

> My mother and father
> My sister, Abigail
> My brothers, David and Steven

## Acknowledgments

I would like to thank Robert K. Massie, for his wisdom as a teacher, his insight as a writer, and his encouragement as a friend. Had I not been in his class and had he not allowed me the freedom to write about what I knew best, this book may not have been.

For not knocking on my door every five minutes while I was trying to write, I thank Nan and Camilla, my roommates and friends. Special thanks to Nan, whose humor and love helped me through it all.

And I thank Bobby, for his consistent faith in my writing, and his fine editorial eye. For his dares, his dreams, and for his love, which gave me hope.

# THE
# DAY
# THE
# LOVING
# STOPPED

# 1

"Welcome to the original nuclear family!" I had written in jubilant letters on the note pad on my door. For the first time since my parents' divorce in April, 1966, my father, my mother, my sister, and I were to be together, just the four of us, to celebrate the night before my graduation from college. My father was to pick up my mother and my sister in New York, and the three of them were going to drive down to meet me to go to the senior prom. I had never been to a prom before, and I wasn't thrilled at the prospect of a thousand kids and all of their aunts, uncles, and grandparents twirling to the music of a disco band. I looked forward to the evening for a different reason. I wanted to see if I could feel what it was like to be a family again. I wanted to experience a mystical connection to these three people, to reestablish the bond that had been broken, painfully, twelve years before. I had hoped I would be able to sense a glimmer of what we could have had if our family had stayed whole.

Perhaps my expectations were too high, or I was looking for what no longer existed. But, like four pieces from different jigsaw puzzles, we did not fit. The life I shared with my mother and sister was quite separate from my relationship with my father. Over the years we had each worked out our own ways of adjusting to the absence of one parent. We continued to feel their presence the way one remembers a missing limb. And suddenly, we were all together, no one was missing. Yet there was no reminiscent spark, no moment I could point to and say, yes, this is what it was like. Instead, my mother was unusually tense, and my father teased her about her mannerisms. It seemed to me that they were instinctively acting the way they used to act when they were married. I introduced my mother and father to my friends as my "parents," a term I had not used in a very long time. All four places at our square table were filled; for once there was no empty chair. I was glad not to have to introduce any stepmothers or girl friends, or explain that "no, they're not married but they live together." Although I had not found even the beginnings of a familiar feeling, at least I knew I could stop looking for it. Whatever we had all lost twelve years ago was truly gone. And what we had now was the pieced-together look of a beautifully shaped vase which has been broken and carefully reglued. The shape was slightly changed and there were noticeable cracks between the places. The next morning I was graduated from college. My mother cried; my father didn't.

After a short marriage at the age of twenty-one to a young, dark-haired girl from Philadelphia, my father was a twenty-seven-year-old divorced man with two small sons when he met my mother in 1952. "He was the most beautiful man you have ever seen," my mother has told me. "His eyes were incredibly blue, and he had this jet black hair." They met as patient and therapist, my mother just out of college. My father was beginning his career, and he must have seemed the perfect man for my mother: handsome and very tall, Jewish and a psychologist. She was full-faced and dark, her skin was fresh; she was beautiful. They had an expensive wedding at my grandparents' house in Long Island. Like the figures on top of their wedding cake they must have stood, silent under the *chupah*, their hands gently clasped. I can imagine their solemn faces, the tears in my grandparents' eyes, my mother's younger brothers fidgeting constantly and suddenly standing still when the groom wrapped his arms around their sister and kissed her.

In pictures I have seen of their wedding I am still shocked to see how they smile at each other, how their eyes secretly connect. My father's young, creaseless face, his smooth white dinner jacket hanging on his lean frame, his perfect teeth, are the first things I notice. My mother, very serious, yet smiling with her red lipstick and Marilyn Monroe mole on her cheek. When I look at these pictures I have the small hope of two parents who maybe once really loved each other. I keep this like a lucky stone, forever.

A year and a half after the wedding, my mother became pregnant with me. She wanted a girl, one who would play Beethoven on the violin and read poetry under the covers when the lights were out, who would cry at the ballet and one day love a man the way she loved my father. She later told me that she had never felt as healthy and alive as when she was pregnant. Her full breasts and growing stomach made her feel rich and proud. I was her first child, my father's third. His sons, my half brothers, were six and four: David, blond and silken; Steven, dark-haired and chubby.

The summer before I was born the four of them lived in Fire Island, my mother's bulging stomach growing unsettled as I kicked at her to let me out. I believe that one reason I am drawn to the ocean is that for the two months before I was born I was rocked to sleep by the sound of the sea.

But I was not a summer baby. I waited for the first day of fall to be born. "Julie Autumn," my father called me, born September 21, 1956. My mother had wanted to call me Cara, or Deirdre; she believed my name would ensure me a romantic life. She settled happily on Julie, after Julie Jordan, the girl in *Carousel*. "Julie Autumn—it would make a great name for a stripper," my father had laughed.

"What if I had been a boy?" I asked my father. "What would you have named me then?"

"We didn't even have a boy's name picked out. We wanted a girl and we got you."

A roly-poly bundle of flesh, I was dark, with my mother's eyes, my father's rich hair. "My little Japanese doll," my father used to say, pinching my chipmunk cheeks under squinty eyes. We lived across the street from Central Park, at 10 West 86th Street. As I got older I would play in the park in my underpants. I remember a picture in my grandfather's enormous black photo album, taped crookedly between a day at the circus and some reddish hair from my first haircut. There I am, with a shy smile and my hair in a ponytail, my arms around three black kids whose braids stuck out like porcupine quills. To go under the sprinkler, they wore dirty T-shirts and shorts, and their teeth shone like stars in the blackness of their faces. All I had on was my white underwear, and my flat chest was young and smooth. I also had a long-standing infatuation with the water fountain in the park. I used to stand on tiptoe on the step, pushing the button and playing with the water for hours, slurping it, gargling and spitting it, standing on one leg and spewing it out, being a fountain myself.

My best friend's name was Cookie Godhome, and she lived in the building next to ours. Her mother dressed her in fancy white dresses to play in the park. I was always smudged and dirty while Cookie rocked daintily on the swings. My mother believed in her own ways of bringing me up, for I never got sick and Cookie had colds all year round.

Our apartment was on the fifteenth floor, and my

mother used to sunbathe on the black roof on hot
New York days. She wore a two-piece bathing suit
fashionable in the late 50s. Her skin glistened with
baby oil, catching the light with a silver reflector. I
had nightmares in that apartment: my clown curtains
billowed furiously at night, bringing the noise and
too-bright lights of New York into my pink room. I
dreamed of sophisticated bats with top hats and canes
posed casually on my windowsill. My windows were
always slightly open, but I never once looked out and
down, fearful that the tuxedoed bat would still be on
the sill, waiting to catch me with his cane.

During one nightmare, herds of buffalo came stam-
peding in my window, running over me and my little
bed with its pink spread. They were furious, fuming.
I pulled the covers over my head but I could still see
them. When the fear was too great I ran into my
mother's and father's room and crawled into bed between them. They were deep in sleep, back to back,
each one hugging a pillow to them like a doll.

"What's wrong?" my mother said, pulling me to
her.

"They're coming, they're coming," and I started
to cry.

They both held me then, until my breathing slowed
and my eyes were dry. There was nothing safer in
the world, no better warmth than the sandwich of
my mother and my father and me, squeezed in between them.

The bed was big and wide, a couch bed with long
bolsters and lots of pillows. When the heavy spread

was pulled down and the pillows thrown on the floor, the blankets and below were a haven. In the morning I brought in my scrawny blond-haired doll and spoke to her, dressing her while my parents slept. I didn't need to wake them, for I felt happy and safe that they were there, together, and with me.

The first four and a half years of my life were filled with small victories and disappointments. At a distant cousin's wedding, I felt lost and abandoned. I grabbed at a pair of long legs I believed to belong to my father, thinking I was finally safe. When the tall man peered down at my hands clutching his pants' legs, it was not my father's face, and I burst into tears, abandoned once more.

At Walden, the "progressive" nursery school I went to, I remember being able to slide down a long fireman's pole, and in kindergarten being amazed that my red-haired teacher made us push in our own chairs. At night I would listen to Danny Kaye records, especially my favorite song, "Mommy, Give Me a Drink of Water." My mother taught me to read. When I was four I sat on her lap on our orange couch and pieced together the words in "A Fly Went By." By this time, I had been taking art classes at the Metropolitan for a year; all of my finger paintings were purple and black, but my mother didn't worry.

My father bought me a kit with dozens of bottles to make perfume, and I would sit cross-legged on the floor in my room, mixing concoctions for hours. The

smells were flowery and artificial, but so distinctive
that even now in certain places I sense them and see
myself on that floor, my father bending down over
me, pretending that they were the most beautiful
things he had ever smelled. My father also spent time
with David and Steven alone, and they stayed with us
often. I took baths with them; I would sit and splash
in the middle, while the two of them sank plastic ships
and rode matchbox trucks up and down their arms.

In the summers we went to Fire Island as a family.
During the year my mother really only had one child.
But in the summers she had three and she loved it. We
were all brown and healthy. I had learned to walk
there, pushing a stroller from behind, drooling, gur-
gling, my pudgy short legs working like those of a stiff
marionette. The pictures of us in Fire Island are idyllic.
My father, his short black hair neatly combed, sitting
at one end of a long log; my two golden brothers in
ironed white shirts and shorts; me, a happy baby,
with bangs and a crooked smile, next to my young
and beautiful mother, her brown legs shapely against
the sand. It is difficult to believe that such harmony
once existed between two people who later could not
force a smile to pass between them.

I was a happy, although serious and shy, little girl.
My hair grew longer until it reached down my back,
and I took to wearing frilly dresses, short white gloves,
and black tights, carrying a fan and a pocketbook
wherever I went, even to the beach. I don't know
where I picked up this affectation; my mother certainly never waved a fan before her face like a blushing

geisha girl. She let me have my way, taking pictures to allow me to believe I was a movie star or a high society woman on my way to tea with the emperor of Japan.

As a rule, I hated having my picture taken because my grandfather used to snap at me constantly with his Polaroid. I wouldn't smile for him at my kinder-garten graduation (wearing a miniature white robe yet), so there is a photograph of twenty smiling five-year-olds and me, refusing to look at the camera, pouting.

But he did capture certain moments: my first pony ride, my mother and me in twin dresses, her hair swept up on her head in a bun, and me, with an identical bun, smiling in her arms. He took one of my mother and father holding me in the park, the two of them grinning proudly as they offered up their prize package. After the divorce, my grandfather took the picture from his kitchen wall and razored my father out, leaving half of my body floating in the air, my mother's grin suddenly looking quite foolish.

One of my favorite pictures is of me sitting back on a couch in one of my white dresses, holding an open-mouthed baby in my arms. My face looks blessed with a simple happiness, my dark eyes shining and somehow deeper than in earlier pictures. It is just 1961 and I have wrapped my hands around the small body of my baby sister, Abigail. My face is glowing.

When Abigail Sara List came home from the hospital, I was suddenly no longer alone on the fifteenth floor. There was a new housekeeper from Georgia,

Josephine, and this baby with eyes like black olives. I used to stand over her crib and grasp her pink fingers; they looked like baby shrimp. She had a noticeable sense of humor; even then she would mug for the camera. This new addition brought our family close together, even though my father had not been at the hospital for my sister's birth. He told my mother he had to go to a "meeting," that the doctor assured him the baby wouldn't come for hours. I wonder now if those were the beginning signs of something wrong. Perhaps, but this new baby made my father very happy, I know that. Abigail means "father's joy," and she has lived up to her name.

One month after my sister was born I said very seriously to my mother, "Okay, I've had enough, you can put her back in now." My mother tried not to laugh and kissed me, assuring me that Abigail was most definitely not going away but was there to stay.

My mother would sing to her, the two of them bobbing up and down like apples in my grandparents' pool in Weston, Connecticut. My grandparents had moved into New York and opened their summer house to us. Abby loved the swings in Central Park, with the cold metal bar that slipped down over her round, pink-snowsuited belly. She never cried when I held her on my lap, and I could smell her Johnson's Baby Powder and clean, special baby smell.

Steven and David, by now eight and ten, were stretching into wild little boys. They lived in a small apartment on 54th Street with their mother. They loved coming to our place and playing with Abigail;

her eyes shone at their attention. On weekends they slept over in the bunk beds we had for them. On those nights a real family slept: a mother, a father, two sons, and two daughters. I was not aware of it then, for I knew nothing else and it seemed perfectly normal. But years later I tried to remember what it felt like and I couldn't.

Soon after the birth of my sister, we moved into a little red house on Blind Brook Road in Westport, Connecticut. For the first year we were there, I insisted on calling it Yesport, which made my father laugh. We had a backyard, pachysandra, and cool brooks to wade in. In the summer I ate watermelon on the front steps with my brothers, spitting out seeds. In the winter I went sledding and once I veered into the rosebushes, cutting my eyelid. I built a world of my house and the one next door. I invented games and performed scientific experiments with Paul, Laura, and Jeremy in the old stone house they lived in. To get there I had to cross a stream on a bridge made of stones that looked like turtle shells. My feet had to land exactly in the center. Abby used to wander into the neighbors' yards, and twice the same dog bit her on her upper lip.

I loved living in the country and believed my mother and father had moved there in order to bring us up in the fresh air, with a yard, a swing set, and trees to climb. Recently I learned that this move had been an effort to try to save the marriage. I didn't know that anything was wrong between these two people, this mother and father who were supposed to be a unit, as permanent a fixture as the double bed in their bedroom. Even here, in the one-floor house where I had no nightmares, where life was as regular as the ringing of the bell on the Good Humor man's truck on summer nights, my mother and father were sensing a kind of irreconcilable "presence." It was then that my father began the search for a bigger house, an older house where he could have an office, where everyone could have their own room, a place for his two sons to visit. Perhaps he thought they could ignore the "presence" in the additional space.

When I was six years old and starting the first grade, I went house hunting with my parents. I don't remember visiting many other houses, but the day we went to see the huge white house on North Sylvan Road stands out very clearly in my mind. We walked slowly through the one-hundred-year-old black-shuttered house, led around by a white-haired couple who were very anxious for us to buy it. There was a butler's pantry and five bathrooms, three fireplaces downstairs and, best of all, a fireplace in the room that Abigail and I were to share. There was an enormous double bed in our room-to-be which was so high I remember not being able to see over it to the other side.

In the front yard there were cherry, pear, and apple trees. The backyard was hilly, a lush green and meticulously tended to, the forsythia a shock of yellow. The couple had designed the house conservatively; all of the wallpaper had different kinds of colorless birds on it. The most exciting thing was a hidden doorway to an attic in the garage. The old man had led me out there and with an arthritic finger pointed up to it, saying, "Now don't you tell your folks about this place. This is your secret." Terrified and thrilled, I vowed I would never tell them, and I looked forward to the first day we moved in so that I could tiptoe up to the secret room.

My father loved the house, the old wood beams in the living room. He had never really lived in a house before, having been brought up in city apartments and hotel rooms. He strode through the rooms like a man who has first learned to use the length of his legs. My mother seemed to love it too, but its size overwhelmed her. She didn't know if she would be able to keep it clean, if the dust would ever leave her alone. We moved in April, and I was to grow up in the house for the next twelve years.

The first year that we lived in our new house my mother and father used the bathroom connected to their bedroom, a small pink room with one sink. But one day I noticed that the guest bathroom had been taken over by my father's own soaps and smells, and I didn't understand.

My mother had always been too messy for my father, which wasn't difficult considering his zeal for cleanliness. Brought up by a mother who wouldn't let him play outside unless his clothes were ironed and starched, my father has always been a compulsive cleaner. In his new bathroom the glass shelves were never dusty or encrusted with powder as my mother's had been, and he must have Windexed the mirror daily. In my mother's shower there were long black hairs stuck in the holes of the drain and thin, odorless bars of used soap in a sticky soap dish. My father's shower was shiny and hair-free. Even after he took a shower he didn't let water droplets gather on the tiles. In his new bathroom all was order, cleanliness, and cologne. His cologne was everywhere, a light, smooth smell that always makes me think of him. After he had been there for a while I would come in some early mornings before school and watch him shave. He always wore his thin bikini underwear while he performed his daily routine. He was never modest before us. I sat on the closed toilet seat, looking up at his face in the mirror, scrutinizing the pathways made by the razor. Fascinated, I asked him if I could do it too, and he let me—without the blade, of course. It was very satisfying, clearing off the lovely billowing shaving cream in smooth strokes, like shoveling snow off a walk, pushing soap off a car windshield.

I didn't question my father's move at the time, even though it seemed peculiar. It was only sometime later when he began sleeping in the guest room that I knew something was different and very wrong.

# 2

The times I remember being with my father most are Christmas and summers. The rest of the time I "heard" him more than I saw him. During our first years in Westport he used to leave very early in the morning to drive to his office in New York. He woke up and performed his morning ritual, often while I was still asleep, but every now and then I could hear him in his new bathroom. He showered with the radio on very loud, and then brushed his teeth furiously, spitting out with a vengeance, a unique sound that only he made. If I listened very carefully I could hear him cleaning his nails with a nailbrush, and the slap, slap, slap as he splashed on his cologne after his silent shave. Some days if he had enough time he would walk quietly down the hallway to our room. He would bend down to kiss my cheek, his tie brushing against my face as he stood up. I always pretended to be asleep, for if he had known I was awake he would have whispered gibberish into my ear until I couldn't breathe for laughing so hard.

Christmas was a time I counted on *seeing* him, for I had known since I was four years old that *my father*, and not every fat, red-suited man with a bell on the street corner, was Santa Claus. Ever since I had glimpsed a trunkload of presents in my father's car, I had known that it was he. Though we were Jewish, we celebrated Christmas every year with chairfuls of presents and stockings stuffed with Hershey's Kisses, Almond Joy bars, decks of cards, and bubble bath, hanging from the mantel. Every year we asked for a tree and each time my mother refused, insisting that the tree was "the most Christian symbol of all" and no Jewish household of hers was going to display one. My father had not been brought up with the same Jewish tradition as my mother and was always on our side. But in those days my mother won and we compromised: we lit the Chanukah candles, singing "Rock of Ages," and my father, as Santa Claus, accepted all letters of request.

On a piece of yellow construction paper, in purple crayon, in a newly learned print (which became sloppier as it went along), I wrote:

Dear Santa Claus (DADDY),
For Christmas I would like:
1. a camera,
2. a pretty large teddy bear,

(dolls) 3. Skipper's, Ken's, and Barbie clothes,
        4. a pair of boots that can be worn with-
        out shoes, some more peanuts (Peanuts
        are like Charlie Brown, you know) and
        a donkey troll
        If it's too much. . . . . . . . . . .
        Oh well. I tried.
            Love Julie
            List

And in the upper-right-hand corner in a box: "Written: Thurs. the 10th 1964."

Christmas Eve was the longest night of the year. Abigail and I were so excited we would count Santa Clauses to make ourselves fall asleep. If that didn't work, we switched to reindeer or popcorn balls; counting sheep seemed inappropriate on Christmas Eve. We woke up at six when it was still dark, the snow glistening on the branches outside our bedroom window. We weren't allowed to wake up our parents until seven, so we would sneak down into the living room, gasping at the presents, the ribbons, the overflowing stockings. When we finally woke them up, they reluctantly put on their bathrobes. My father in slippers, my mother barefoot, they accompanied us into toyland. One year Abby gave my father a stuffed koala bear, and with my new Instamatic I took a picture of him, looking groggy and wrinkled, holding up the grinning animal.

# 3

After a year of living in our new house, Abigail and I requested that our two single beds be placed one on top of the other to make bunk beds. David and Steven had bunk beds and we envied them. At the time it seemed a more adventurous way of living, and I loved climbing things, reaching my kingdom six feet above everything else. One morning I woke up and, wanting to rush to the window to see if it had snowed the night before, jumped off my top bunk, not looking where my feet were to land. Suddenly there was a sharp pain in the big toe of my right foot. I sat down on the floor quickly and saw that a sewing needle had gone in one side of my toe and come out the other side. I was terrified at the sight of it and began screaming, waking Abby. "Go get Isabel, hurry, Ab," I cried. Isabel was our Scottish housekeeper, a young girl who slept downstairs in a room off the kitchen. Isabel came panting up the stairs, tying her robe around her.

"Oh my God," she whispered. "What have you done to yourself?" she asked in her accent. I held up the skewered toe, not quite believing that it had really happened. Flustered, she called behind her, "I'll go get your father."

Abby and I sat in the middle of the floor, and tears fell down my cheeks. My father came, finally, in his bathrobe. Without a word he took my foot in his hands and yanked out the needle in one movement, the way you're supposed to pull off a Band-Aid. He held it up to the light, a prize specimen. Pulling me onto his lap, he massaged my foot around the punctured toe, which did not even bleed. Isabel looked relieved. About this time my mother sleepily wandered in, the back of her blue robe unzipped, pushing her glasses up on her nose.

"What happened?" she asked, lying down on Abby's lower bunk.

"Julie was doing a little early-morning sewing," my father said, winking at me.

I smiled at my father. He had rescued me.


My father had a knack for pulling out things which didn't belong. I was eight and my baby teeth were finally beginning to fall out. Our family was slow with teeth; they didn't start to poke through our gums until we were nearly two, and my mother would rub Scotch on them when we cried. We didn't lose these slowly earned baby teeth until all of our friends had almost complete sets of grown-up teeth. One of my front teeth was giving me a particularly hard time: it refused to fall out; it wiggled back and forth like a stick shift between gears. One day my father offered to pull it out for me, to end my continual wiggling and give me a nice space in the front of my mouth.

I was afraid. "How did Steven lose his baby teeth? Didn't they just fall out if he waited long enough?"

"He didn't need to wait. David knocked them out for him when they were wrestling on the bed. Steven had to wait two years before the new front teeth grew in."

I didn't know if that story was supposed to make me feel better or worse, but I decided it would be smarter for me to get it pulled out than punched out. So my father sat on the closed toilet seat in his bathroom and tied a piece of dental floss around the tooth. I held on to the sink. "Can't you give me a bullet to bite on, Daddy?" and yank! it was gone. The little tooth sat like a pearl in the palm of my father's hand.

"Do I get to put this under *my* pillow tonight?" he asked. "Since I pulled it out—"

I was examining the new space in the front of my mouth, exploring it with my tongue.

"No, Daddy," I said. "Because *you* are the tooth fairy!"

That tooth brought me a dollar the next morning. I usually got a quarter, but I think my bravery helped.


There were Sunday mornings when my mother and father read the *New York Times*, listening to classical music, padding around the house in their bathrobes until late afternoon. There were Barbra Streisand Sundays, when they would play all of her records. Sometimes my father would help me with my math homework, because my mother still couldn't add or subtract in her head. "Look, I only got a circle 65 on my geométry regents—I barely passed. Ask your father, Julie," she would say. "He knows about those things."

My father and I played the piano together occasionally on Sundays. The only song he knew was: "I knew a girl from Syracuse, she got drunk on lemon juice. On the way home she raised the deuce, just because her pants were loose." My father taught me that while I was supposed to be practicing Czerny exercises for my piano lesson. He loved our piano, which had been my mother's as a little girl. My father and I played for hours, making up songs and composing masterpieces.

In addition to wanting to be a famous pianist, I wanted to be a ballerina. I could tell my father thought it would be nice if I became one too.

"Dear Daddy," I wrote, "I am in love with someone. His initials are M.D.L.Ph.D. Guess who. Love Punkin." And he wrote: "I'm flattered, honored, proud—and besides all that jazz—it's great to have as my Punkin someone like you—whose initials happen to be J.A.L.—my future prima ballerina and dancing partner. Love, Daddy-O."

I could see myself in a pink tutu made out of the material that looked like it had been sprinkled with glitter, covered at the bottom with crepelike frills.

My mother found ballet classes for me and we shopped for the tiny black slippers that had to have strips of black elastic over the widest part of the foot. In class I lined up along the bar with all of the other ballerinas-to-be, my hair bouncing on my back in two long braids. I watched my short legs trying to point and stretch in the mirror; the rest of the girls were blessed with long, thin legs which obeyed their commands.

"Round your elbow, Julie," Miss DeBergh would tell me. "And don't look so serious."

Hurriedly changing after class, I would run outside, hoping to find my mother waiting, but she was never there. My mother was late everywhere she went. After every class I have ever taken, whenever I was finished with school, my mother would appear fifteen minutes late, zooming around the corner in her dented green station wagon, a swift apology always on hand. "Right when I was leaving the dishwasher broke down," or "Your sister couldn't find her brush and I had to look through all her drawers before I found it behind the radiator."

I lost interest in Miss DeBergh's classes because I thought she was trying to turn all of us into miniature prima donnas. I switched to Mr. Volodine, a Russian whose long arms and legs and polished bald head gave him the look of a joker in a deck of cards. His class terrified me from the start, but my desire to become a ballerina was so great that I decided to stick it out. However, after weeks of polkas and square dances even my father agreed with me when I said that this wasn't what I had had in mind. Mr. Volodine was finished for me when he teased me about my red tights looking like pajamas. He had turned off the polka music and, directing his piercing eyes at me, asked, "Deed you forget to shange your close thees morning, Julie?" All of the other kids stared at me, ready for me to have a good crying episode or to come to my defense. I came home that day and at dinner told my mother and father that I wanted to stop taking ballet lessons.

"I'm sorry, Julie," my mother said from her seat at one end of the dining room table, "I won't let you be a quitter. You'll have to continue. He can't be that bad."

"Don't be ridiculous," said my father. "If she's unhappy there, what's the point?"

I played with the wax dribbling down the side of the candles in the center of the table. Abby pushed her peas around in circles on her plate, finally hiding them under a mound of cold mashed potatoes when she thought no one was looking.

"I don't want her to go through life as a quitter. She's got to learn now that some things have got to be seen through. I'm sorry—she can't just drop them now."

"Your attitude is unbelievable," my father said, looking at her with his mouth slightly open, a look which I knew meant disappointment. "I don't know where you pick up these ideas."

I sat still in my chair, feeling as though I were watching a heated tennis match.

I did leave Mr. Volodine's class, but that argument

at the dinner table had confused me. Both my mother and father seemed different when they spoke like that. My mother's face became tight and small, and my father's voice was loud and slow. Abigail and I didn't say anything to each other after that dinner, but in our room that night we didn't fall asleep right away.

"Ab?" I whispered.

"Yeah?"

"Are you okay?"

There was a pause, and then, "Yeah. I'm glad I don't want to be a belly dancer."

I tried not to laugh. "Ball*et* dancer."

"Oh. Yeah. G'night."

# 4

When I entered the fourth grade, our lives began to take on an entirely new routine. All of the good things started to disappear, and they were replaced with the awareness that everything was slightly off kilter.

In many ways, I have blocked out the life that existed before this time. It is as though my first signs of consciousness are directly linked to the times I remember being unhappy. The contrast between the good and the bad was so evident, I believe now that in order to spare myself the pain of knowing what I had lost, I allow myself only snatches of good memories.

I rarely let myself remember and actually *feel* how much I loved my father then. It is only when I see the Father's Day cards I gave him, addressed to "my darling Daddy" or to "the perfect Daddy," that pieces of these memories come back to me. He called me

"Pungin," a takeoff on "Punkin," the name of the stuffed animal he had given me one birthday. I signed all my early cards with this name. It was our secret. I see the two of us snuggled close to each other on the bed in my brothers' room, watching "The Man from U.N.C.L.E." on TV. My head is on my father's chest, his hands stroking my long hair. We always used to watch television together on Monday nights my father has told me.

In retrospect, my father made brief but clear appearances into my life, and the day-to-day participation is nearly forgotten. He picked me up from school one day when he arrived home early from work. He owned a beige Karmann Ghia that year, and as I ran out the school's front doors into the arms of my father in his snazzy little car, I was very proud.

I remember one winter's night while Abigail and I were lying in our beds. We heard heavy breathing coming from somewhere in our room. We cried out to our mother but she didn't believe us. After an hour of frightened wailing my father strode down the long hallway to our room and stood for a moment, listening. He agreed that there was indeed a noise. Abby and I jumped into one bed, sitting very still and waiting for him to discover the body under our beds. Approaching the chimney, my father shone a flashlight up there and found a bewildered raccoon, stuck halfway. My father let us sleep in our brothers' empty beds that night, and my mother called the exterminator the next day. We considered our father an ally.

# 5

My father used to invite his mother to spend weekends with us in the country. Before she was married her name had been Sara Silver; we called her Grandma Sallie.

I never met my grandfather because he and my grandmother had divorced before my parents were married. He remarried a woman named Helen, who to me is only a bright smile and silver sprayed hair in pictures. My father and his father did not speak to each other for eight years, and my grandfather died in 1967. So I never knew him. But Grandma Sallie made a lasting impression on me.

She lived in an apartment on 54th Street for as long as I had known her, in the same building as my brothers and their mother. It didn't occur to me then, but it was definitely a single woman's apartment.

There were no traces of a man: no shaving cream or cologne on the bathroom shelves, no ties or slippers. She had a large double bed, two dressers, and an exerciser by the window, a long bendable table which was supposed to massage her back while folding her up in impossible positions. Sometimes when Grandma Sallie was in the kitchen and couldn't hear, I would turn on the machine and watch its wavelike movements. With no body on it, it had an eerie life of its own. On her dressing table were rows of perfume bottles, and in the drawers were piles of empty duplicates. There were nail files, cuticle scissors, and several colors of nail polish from which to choose. She had a large television facing her bed. It sat like an open eye in the center of the room. Her favorite show was Lawrence Welk; I think she liked the bubbles.

In Grandma Sallie's living room there were white chairs with plastic slipcovers and an oversized, out-of-tune piano in one corner of the room. Sitting on the piano was a stuffed white cat, its green glass eyes gleaming. When Abby and I came to visit, that cat, or one exactly like it, looked at us as though it were alive. This was perhaps due to the fact that sometimes when we came it was sprawled on the piano and other times sitting in a bored manner on the dresser in Grandma Sallie's bedroom. We later found out that whenever it looked too dirty from her four grandchildren's handling or if the tail had fallen off, Grandma Sallie would buy another one and put it in the old one's original place. At the time we thought the same one lived forever. Also on the piano was a photograph of my father and his sister when they were very young. My father was wearing a sailor suit, and his black hair was combed flat against his head. His sister had a demure look; her hand barely touched her brother's shoulder.

There were glass jars of colored sour balls on a small table in the living room and an enormous armoire against one wall. Whenever we wanted to play cards (we were all card sharks in this family) Grandma Sallie would gingerly swing wide the doors of the armoire and reveal to us the pictures of her sour-faced parents, her surviving graying sisters, and several decks of worn cards. Every time we wanted to play casino we had to listen to a story about one of Grandma Sallie's ancestors.

At night Grandma Sallie made us boiled chicken and then used the same thin, undernourished bird to make a watery chicken soup. We did not love Grandma Sallie for her cooking. The chicken looked as though it were still alive and merely wet. Its yellow skin hung off the bones like the flesh from an old woman's arm. The vegetables in the soup were tasteless, so when Grandma Sallie returned to her narrow kitchen for the mashed potatoes, we poured half of the salt shaker's contents into our chicken-flavored water. The limp noodles lay on the bottom of the bowl like strips of wet paper. We pretended to love Grandma Sallie's chicken and soup, so she made it every time, especially for us.

When Abby and I came to visit her there was one event we always waited for. Every night before she went to sleep, Abby and I would climb up into her double bed and wait for her to come out of the bathroom in her nightgown. We could see her long breasts sagging under it, and her waist-length dark red hair was still up on her head in a bun. Sitting on the edge of the bed, her slippers dangling off her feet, she pulled out the pins until the coil of her hair fell about her shoulders, covering her breasts. Taking a wooden brush, she lovingly brushed her hair, its auburn lights catching the faint glow from her bedside lamp. Then, slowly, she would divide the hair into three sections, her long polished fingernails occasionally snagging on a strand of hair, and braid it, placing one section over the other. Abby and I watched silently and wondered if our hair could ever be that long, that red and thick. Once finished, she slipped under the covers and turned off the light. The three of us fit perfectly into one bed, although whoever was in the middle had to stay in the same position for most of the night. In the dark, the still white exerciser lay like a body ready for burial, its legs dull gray in the night. We listened to the sounds of New York until we fell asleep.

In the mornings Grandma Sallie had gravelly breath, and sometimes I would spy on her in the bathroom when she sat on the toilet for long periods of time. This was the only time Grandma Sallie smoked cigarettes. Through the keyhole I could watch her thin breasts hanging, the smoke from her cigarette surrounding her. Later when I went in there the smell of stale smoke and bowel movement mingled to produce a coarse odor.

Grandma Sallie visited us in Westport, and it was there I learned how she used to rub my arms for hours with lotion when I had had eczema at four. My father told me that Grandma Sallie had taken good care of me then and prevented me from scratching my peeling arms which eventually had to be wrapped in casts. From that time on, I had a special feeling for Grandma Sallie for I knew she really loved me. Her birthday was a week before mine, so I felt we were kindred spirits. One day I took the Instamatic camera I had gotten for Christmas and posed Grandma Sallie on the bed in my mother's and father's room. She was wearing a bright green dress, and her hair was tightly wrapped on her head. Sitting with her legs crossed, her thin hands folded over her knees, she smiled, and I caught her image, to remember her like that forever. When her beautiful hair was cut off to her ears and gray, I could still envision her in that green dress, her face shining under the crown of her hair.

One night during the time when things were not going very well between my mother and father, Grandma Sallie was baby-sitting for Abigail and me. My parents had gone to a party, and Grandma Sallie and I were sleeping in the double bed in the guest room. I had just fallen asleep and Grandma Sallie lay gently snoring beside me. We were awakened by the sound of loud voices at the foot of the stairs. My mother was crying and my father's voice commanded her to stop, to climb the stairs and "get some sleep." Grandma Sallie peered over at me to see if I was still asleep, but I couldn't even pretend. I put my hands between my knees and curled into a ball, listening, yet not wanting to hear. My mother screamed, a sound I had never heard before, and she beat her fists against my father's chest. He became very calm, as though he were dealing with a hysterical child. "Stop it! Just stop it! You'll wake up the whole house," he whispered fiercely.

I heard thuds against his hard body, ineffectual, and her broken wails. "I can't get through!" she cried, and that made her crumple to the floor. My father lifted her up and carried her into their room. He slept in my brothers' empty room, and from the next night until he left he slept in the guest room.

Grandma Sallie stroked my hair until my tears stopped, and the only sound we could hear was my mother's heavy breathing. Years later my mother told me she had been very drunk, something she wasn't used to doing, and didn't even remember what their fight had been about. Grandma Sallie never mentioned what we had overheard; both of us treated it like a brief but disturbing nightmare.

# 6

Although David and Steven were my half brothers, and we saw them only half of the time, I thought of them as my real brothers and they treated me as older brothers do: they teased me, hit my arms, and pinned me to the floor with their knees. Once Steven put his fingers on two points on my throat and said, "If I pressed here hard enough, I could make you faint." He was always letting me in on the way he thought life really worked.

Whenever I visited Grandma Sallie, I would visit them also and read *MAD* magazines while listening to their records. I didn't go there often because they preferred to visit us in Westport. They came as a team, on the 5:57 on Friday nights. We picked them up in our old green station wagon and brought them home to North Sylvan Road. What they did during the

week was a mystery to me; it never occurred to me
that they went to different schools than we did and had
their own friends.

In their room, David, being the elder, slept on the
top bunk and Steven on the bottom. We made houses
by connecting the two beds with blankets. We used
flashlights and spun them around so they looked like
fireflies inside our "tent." It was dark and cozy and we
each had our favorite quilt.

I wanted to marry Steven. He was my ideal. We
were alike: we both cried at the slightest teasing;
loved adventures, secrets, and chemical experiments.
Steven found chemicals in little blue bottles and hid
them in the cracks of the well in our front yard, not
telling anyone but me. One time Steven and I took our
blue quilts and pink blankets and camped out in the
backyard. We found a small spot under some brambles
with enough room for two. We told ghost stories and
scrunched way down in our sleeping bags. He was a
city boy and this was the life for him. I figured it was
all right to want to marry my brother, because he
wasn't my *real* brother. It seemed natural to me that
we didn't have the same mother; his lived in New
York and mine in Westport.

David was different. He was older, and I only saw
him cry once, when my father yelled at him. He wore
straight-legged white pants that came down to his
ankles, white socks, and loafers. He could bend his
fingers at the first joint, and he would curl down all
of them at once, frightening Abby and me. On Sunday
mornings we watched "Wonderama," making balls

out of white bread. Mashing and flattening the dough in our hands, we rolled the little circles and threw them at each other. Sometimes David and I would lie on his upper bunk, watching "Outer Limits." Every now and then when there was a commercial he would pounce on me, tickle me, and say in a devilish voice, "Now what shall we do with the Julie-bird?" For many years I wondered what horrible answer he was going to come up with. Once Steven and I spied on David from the bathroom; we saw him kiss his first girl friend. We were still young enough to think it was gross and funny, and we teased him for weeks.

Sometimes the three of us set off cherry bombs in the backyard. I was frightened, yet they seemed to know what they were doing. We played Spud, and handball in the garage. They let me win on occasion, but usually they liked to show off their strength. I told them about the secret room in the garage and we stole up there early one Saturday morning. It was a long narrow room full of cobwebs and crates. We cleared away the spiders and pretended we were the Munsters. We had ghoulish tea parties that my parents never knew about.

In the summers my mother and father took us to Longshore Club, and we raced around the big pool. The caretaker of the women's locker room was old and had a mustache. She pinned her braids around her head and never wore anything but a gray uniform and black shoes. Her name was Anna, and she sat on a stool outside the changing room, her expression fixed. Longshore was another home for us, because we were free to do whatever we wanted while my mother and father played tennis. Sometimes during a break from our shuffleboard games we would peek through the wire of the tennis court. There was one summer when my father yelled at my mother a lot, accusing her of being too slow when they played doubles, of hitting too hard when the ball went out. I thought my mother was a good player. Her little skirt bounced up and down as she ran after the ball. Sometimes her glasses fell off in midgame, and my father would yell about that. I decided I didn't like my father because he was mean to my mother. In their other fights I couldn't figure out who was right, but here it seemed like he was trying to embarrass her in front of the other couple. Her face would turn very red and I knew he had gone too far. I disappeared to the tether ball, slamming it around and around its pole as hard as I could. Steven and David would come and get me, and we played four-square until it was time to go. I was proud of my brothers; they were tan and strong and winners in sports.

Steven was smart and able to fix anything, an electrical whiz kid. David wanted to be a drummer, then he changed his mind and took up jazz piano. He would drum his fingers on the edge of the dining room table until my father told him to stop—that he was driving him crazy. Steven made sounds when he chewed and my father yelled at him. He hated loud chewing, cracking bubble gum, and sloppy eating. Once Steven picked his nose and ate it and my father smacked him, the only time either of them ever did either of those things. My mother's mother made Steven and David call her "Anne" and wouldn't allow them to call her Grandma, as Abigail and I did.

My grandmother was a psychologist, my grandfather a film producer. For years they had attended the Cannes Film Festival and my grandfather always returned with envelopes full of pictures of movie stars. The majority of them were in bikinis with their arms around his shoulders. In each one he looks well-tanned, his bald pate shining between tufts of white curly hair. He wears a star sapphire ring on his pinky.

They bought the house in Weston to have a place to spend weekends in the country. We would visit them often. Any time of year my grandfather would stock a bowl in his living room full of candy. We four kids would give our hello kisses and rush to see if he had surprised us with Mounds bars or Mary Janes, Nestlé's Crunch or Good & Plenty. Then he would take us down the long hallway where he had covered an entire wall with famous people he had encountered in his career. Sean Connery, Vanessa Redgrave, Eleanor Roosevelt, and John Barrymore smiled out at us. Whenever we had friends over, Grandpa would give us the tour of the wall, knowing how impressed we were.

My grandfather spoke very loudly and he believed he was right about everything. My grandmother, after swimming laps in her bikini, would clear the lunch table, dipping the Kleenex, which she kept up her sleeve, into water before rubbing out a spot of dried gravy or orange juice. There was a tension around them when we were there and, on occasion, loud fights.

My father didn't always come with us since he didn't get along with my grandparents. He was strong-willed and opinionated, and my grandparents didn't agree with many of his viewpoints, especially those concerning their daughter. I didn't sense anything wrong; I just slapped around in my flip-flops, sucked on pink Popsicles, and looked through Grandpa's photo albums. There were pictures of my grand-mother when she was young; she didn't look any older now. She had inherited her mother's smooth white Russian skin, soft like the underside of rose petals.

Steven, David, and I swam in the pool, having races with my uncles. There were days when we wouldn't get out and my mother tried to convince us that our fingers would look like prunes for life. We ate the special chicken and cole slaw that their housekeeper, Rita, made and threw pebbles at the frogs in the pond.

Uncle Peter and I had an ongoing story between us. Whenever I came he filled me in on the next install-ment. He said he knew a man who lived at the bottom of their swimming pool named Mr. Crampton. "He wears a bowler derby and he always smokes a cigar," Uncle Peter would say. "And sometimes he loosens his bow tie if it is pinching his throat." For a long time it seemed perfectly normal to me that Mr. Crampton lived on the bottom of the pool. But as I got older I sensed something peculiar.

"How can his cigar stay lit under water?" I asked

Uncle Peter, sure that I had finally stumped him.

"He has to relight it from time to time," he said knowingly, "but he doesn't mind just chewing on it if he runs out of matches."

Steven and David would walk away in disgust, but I adored our Mr. Crampton stories.

My mother loved Steven and David. She treated them like her own sons, and kissed them and made sure they had what they needed. She had always wanted to have sons, she said. She was happy with her two daughters, but she had a fantasy about little red-haired boys with freckles and glasses. Steven and David didn't have any of those things, but she loved them anyway.

# 7

I wanted to be a stewardess when I grew up. At first I thought it was pronounced "studeress," and I imagined it had something to do with being a student in the sky. I loved school, and the idea that I could have notebooks, pencil cases, and millions of books every day was something to look forward to. No one else loved school the way I did. Once I tricked my mother into letting me go even when I had the mumps; I refused to miss a day. School meant many friends and handball with the boys at recess. It was writing short stories and pretending my name was Julietta for an entire year. If we were too talkative, Mrs. Banks would put us "out in space," moving our desks away from everyone else's so that no one could talk to us. I cried often then, an easy target for flirtatious and sometimes cruel little boys. At night in my bed I would talk out loud to myself, recapitulating with those who had hurt me during the day. My mother told me later that some nights she and my father stood outside my door, listening. "Okay, Julie," I would say to my left hand. Because I was left-handed I thought my left hand was an adequate representation of me. My right was the enemy, the inevitable loser. "Let's see what you can do." And the two hands would wrestle.

"Julie wins!" I would cry, glancing quickly over to Abby, making sure I hadn't woken her up. "That was very good, Julie," I whispered. "You showed 'em all right."

Another thing I thought about when I was nine had to do with a misconception about God. When I thought of God, I saw a man in a bathing suit and white hat with a red line around the brim. He flew through the air, but felt most at home on a beach. As a matter of fact, he looked almost exactly like the young men who sit on high white chairs facing the ocean, scanning the waves for drowning swimmers. "Life guard" and "God" were intermingled in my mind, and I thought I knew exactly what God looked like. This explanation so satisfied me that I didn't question the existence or the manifestation of God. But when people would say to me, "God is everywhere," I had a difficult time understanding how He could be in so many places at once. After all, there weren't millions of little "life Gods" swimming through the air; there was just one, with short blondish hair who looked a lot like a Ken doll. Soon I expanded my vision of God. If He was everywhere, that meant He was a big face which covered the circle of the earth. Just as the earth has three dimensions, depth, and substance, so did God's face fill every millimeter of our world. Sometimes I wondered which part of His nose or eyebrow was in me.

We didn't discuss God much in our early family. I never told anyone my ideas about Him until much later when I realized my first intuitions may not have been just right. It didn't seem like such a serious business until I realized that God and being Jewish were related. We had always gone to synagogue on the High Holidays, and my mother tried sending us to Sunday school, but I don't ever remember going to synagogue with my father, even during the good times. I wonder if this was a source of pain for my mother. I have no vision of him reading from the prayer book or singing the Hebrew songs. At no Passover service do I see his face among the recliners. I only remember pictures of him at my grandparents' house in New York, a yarmulke on his head for the Friday night dinner.

As the fighting between my mother and father increased, his participation in these occasional Friday night dinners diminished. After a while he simply stopped coming. My mother made excuses for him, but I think my grandparents were suspicious. When my father didn't come, I wore his yarmulke.

Before my parents' divorce, I didn't know much about my father's life in New York, his work, his friends, or how he spent all those hours away from us.

After a year of substitute teaching high school English, my mother had started working part-time at the town newspaper, the *Westport News*. I went to see her often at the office, where she began her career writing feature stories.

I remember one Saturday morning visiting my father in his office. It was the first time I had ever seen this part of his world. It was unnaturally quiet. His shelves were lined with thick professional books. There was a diamond-shaped mosaic on one wall which he could fill with light by turning a switch. He had a tiger lamp that a patient had given him and, best of all, an old green globe that lit up, illuminating the continents. The globe was a present from his father in 1945. It fascinated me, and I spun it around and around, tracing Africa, China, Australia with my finger. On his desk my father had a large sheet of glass, and underneath it were pictures of his four children. I wondered if he glanced over at us from time to time when he was bored with his patients' stories. To the left of his desk was a small safe, and I asked him if I could see what was inside. Quietly he turned the dial, listening for the right sounds. He showed me my birth certificate, old letters, money, and official documents. Later my father kept his divorce papers in there. In his bathroom even the Kleenex was mysteriously scented. The whole place *was* my father.

The year I became nine I noticed that my father was coming home from work later and later. Tuesdays had always been his "late days." He never came home before ten o'clock because the group therapy sessions he led weren't over until nine and then he had to drive home. When the fighting between my mother and father occurred more frequently, there were nights when he didn't come home at all. Wednesdays and Thursdays suddenly became "late days" too. My mother said to us, "Your father has a lot of work to do, and he does it better at night." He told us he slept in the fold-out couch in his office if he was too tired to drive home.

"Aren't you lonely, Daddy?" I asked.

"No, don't worry. I'm so tired I don't know where I am," he'd say, not looking me in the eye.

I don't remember my father walking in the back door after work at night. I have no image of him slipping off his overcoat or stamping on the mat to loosen snow from his shoes. I can recall the four of us at the dinner table, eating steak and baked potatoes, and salad with the vinegary dressing my father and I loved. All of my mother's and father's greatest fights were conducted from their two chairs at each end of our dining room table. Perhaps with Abigail and me present they knew their *true* feelings would not completely surface. We were, in a sense, their safety valve, because for every fight there was a "not in front of the children" implied. The yelling matches at the dinner table were tense and painful. Some nights they hurled insults back and forth as though aiming darts for the bull's-eye. Abigail and I always sat in the middle, looking at our plates, sometimes letting our feet comfort each other under the table.

One night I said that I wanted to stop taking piano lessons. I complained that I had too much homework and too little free time and that I wasn't getting any better. They had the "quitter" argument, but this time my mother refused to budge. I felt her anger was directed at me, although she looked at my father. She disapproved of me for wanting to quit, but she was disappointed in him for not seeing beyond the moment. "Years from now, she'll regret this," my mother said. She was right.

During these fights at the dinner table, I almost always cried. Abigail didn't; she sat very still and bit her nails, pulling everything in. I wanted to hide under the table. Night after night I squeezed out of my chair and charged up the back stairs, slamming my door behind me.

The last year before the divorce is a time I have pushed so far away that only images return. My mother cried a lot, her mascara smudging and her glasses slipping down her nose. The sound of my mother's crying was perhaps more painful to me than anything else. I had first seen her cry in our apartment in New York while she was reaching for some canned food from the cabinet. I didn't know why she was crying, and she didn't try to hide it from me. My mother has never pretended to be anything she isn't. Now her crying came from the other side of her bedroom door. It was the sound of a woman in mourning. Sometimes I would knock timidly on her door and she would rock me in her arms. She was getting thinner; her hipbones pressed into my stomach.

On my mother's birthday in September of that year, my father gave her a pair of left-handed scissors. She looked as though she wanted to stab him with them. Then she walked out the back door and stood behind the garage. I followed her. I didn't understand why that was the only present he had given her. I had given her a thick hardback book, the kind she loved. She had kissed me and licked me in the ear until I begged her to stop. When she turned around she saw me watching her behind the garage. Her mascara had made black lines down her cheeks. She put her hand through mine and we walked back into the house. My father was gone. He had left to play tennis.

I don't know what my mother and father were fighting about. But it was a constant in my life. I still loved my father; I didn't think of him as a villain, but I felt protective of my mother. Even so, I continued to give him loving birthday cards, Father's Day cards.

My father lived in the guest room now, when he was home. Steven and David came less often, and our four trees in the front yard went unclimbed. When I climbed mine I felt lost, alone. Our tree house was empty, and I could almost climb the huge tree without my brothers' boosts. Things were changing too quickly.

One of the last family functions I remember going to was the wedding of our Scottish housekeeper, Isabel. She was marrying Dennis, a salesman from Bridgeport. Although I was happy for her, I hated to see her go because she had been like an older sister to Abigail and me. She wanted a life of her own and babies to take care of that belonged to her.

My mother and father, Steven and David and Abigail and I put on our best- and least-loved clothes to go to the wedding. I dressed quickly and was the first one ready, so I sat on the closed toilet seat in my mother's bathroom while she spent twenty-five minutes "putting on her face."

My mother is very nearsighted and the black lines she drew around her eyes were not always straight; the eye shadow she brushed on was thick in some places, invisible in others. As she opened the cabinet mirror in readiness for her mascara, her mouth opened slightly, her eyes looked up at the now curling eyelashes. This was a routine I never tired of, although my favorite part was the red lipstick. After making a few faces at herself in the mirror (sometimes for my benefit, often for her own), my mother lined her lips with the red, rubbing them one on top of the other to spread the color evenly. Then she would take a piece of Kleenex (or if none was available, typing paper) and kiss it between her lips, blotting it. On the Kleenex was the perfect shape of a kiss; sometimes my mother signed her letters to me like that, too. Once she was finished, she put her blue-tinted glasses on and no one could see her eyes anyway.

My father didn't take long to get ready, for his clothes were all perfectly pressed and laid out ahead of time. His drawers were lined with scores of clean button-down shirts to choose from and his ties hung neatly in his closet. Pairs of shoes sat side by side in rows, and his jackets hung with just the right amount of space between each one in order to avoid wrinkling. In his thin strapped underwear my father shaved, brushed his teeth, cleaned his nails, and then slapped his face with cologne. I could hear that sound as I sat in my mother's bathroom.

David and Steven combined getting ready with a good pillow fight. Steven had begun his process by lying on his bed in his socks and underwear, reading a science fiction book. He loved science fiction and refused to read anything else. David snuck up on him from behind and walloped him with a pillow. The two of them wrestled for a while until my father's tall figure stood in the doorway. He didn't have to say anything. They knew he was there. They finished dressing after that.

I had to help Abby get dressed because she panicked if she couldn't find the right things. Locating a pair of underpants and an undershirt was often impossible; her drawers had no order to them. No two items of the same category could be found in any one drawer. I searched through the mess until I came up with what she needed, only to find that I now had to find a pair of matching white socks. Abby didn't like brushing her teeth in those days, and she always had a leftover mustache of Hawaiian Punch from dinner the night before. Her hair was short and straight, and she had bangs in her eyes all day long. Abigail lost every brush that was ever given to her. My mother bought her a new one once every two weeks. After three days it was in the kitchen, and by the end of the week in the tree house or next to the well. On this day I took my own wooden brush and sat Abby down before the mirror.

The wedding was very simple. We sat at the children's table at the reception. My mother and father sat with the bride and groom. My father didn't pay much attention to my mother; he enjoyed flirting with the ladies, impressing them with his booming voice, his blue eyes. Pictures were taken, smiles put on, last hugs and kisses given. Isabel put her arms around my shoulders and I cried. She told me I'd always be her wee little sister and that I'd come to see them on weekends in Bridgeport. Someone took our picture while I was crying. I was very embarrassed, humiliated, that my last moment with Isabel was captured on film. Her leaving was the first in a series of separations.

Our next housekeeper's name was Barbara, and she was from England. Abby and I loved her immediately, and our feelings for Isabel faded a bit. Barbara had been with us for about three months in 1965 when we decided that we needed a dog, after the disappearance of our beagle, Poppy, three years before. Barbara, Abby, and I drove to the Humane Society. It was a terrible sight, dogs of all breeds, sizes, and personalities in metal cages with nowhere to run. There was one puppy who kept jumping up and licking us through the bars. "Mixed collie" it said above her cage. She was small and black with deep brown eyes. Her chest was white with flecks of brown. No other dog was as affectionate or as lively; the rest had probably given up long ago. We bought her for nine dollars and drove home. I named her Smokey.

Barbara loved Smokey, and the two of them went for long walks. Whenever Abby and I returned from school, Smokey would bound over to meet us, jumping up and licking our faces. Smokey was the most happiness our house had seen for a while.

My father barely had the chance to know Smokey. There is one picture where my father, Steven, David, Abigail, and I are playing with her in the front yard. Whoever snapped the picture caught us in motion, one rubbing the dog, one pulling hair out of his eyes. We are all smiling and I am proudly holding on to my father's arm. My father is in his element, with the broadest grin of all. He loved being in pictures with his four children. I believe he thought it said something about him, the father of four.

Soon after this picture was taken things began deteriorating badly. No one said anything to me, yet I sensed that something was going to happen. One day I had a bad cold and was recuperating in my mother's bed. I had a fever and Barbara told me to take two Bufferin instead of my usual one. I refused, insisting that I was too young, that two would make me more ill. I cried and called my mother at the newspaper where she worked. After I had taken two aspirin, Barbara asked what was really wrong, why I had cried like that. I thought she already knew, but I told her about my mother's and father's fights, about his staying away so much, about how everything was changing. She sat on the edge of the bed and told me that the same thing had happened with her parents, that her father was a drinker who was very mean to her mother. As she spoke she cried a little, saying that her little brother didn't even remember living with her father and that her memories of him were clouded with her own pain.

"Did you still love your father after he left?" I asked.

"Oh, yes. But after he moved out we never had a real family again. Even so, whatever it was after was better than the fighting and carrying on before."

I was little comforted by Barbara's story. I lay in my mother's bed, waiting for spring.

# 8

My mother finally told us. My sister was five and I was nine. We stood in the hall between the bathroom and our bedroom, looking down, peeling wallpaper, waiting for it to be over. My mother wore little makeup that day and her dark hair fell to her shoulders. She said we were ready to know that things were not going well between them; they had decided that even separate bedrooms had not helped. They needed to be further away from each other, she said, so my father was going to move to New York. Her voice was gentle as she held our small hands in her cool ones and said that both of them would always love us, no matter what. We didn't cry then. We ran down the stairs and out the back door, letting it slam hard behind us.

The morning after my mother told me, I got off the school bus and grabbed my best friend Jacqui's arm.

I said the word for the first time, *divorce*, and with it came the tears, falling in the middle of the four-square court. Girls in knee socks played hopscotch as Jacqui put her arm around my shoulders and let me cry. We were going to count the days of the three months until he left, knowing that after that there would be no more numbers, ever.

Later that week I found out that Barbara's grandfather in London had died. She was to return to England in three months. Taking a black Magic Marker upstairs to my Peanuts calendar, I circled April 6 and April 9, the two dates of departure.

I have found a Valentine's Day card in the bottom of my father's drawer. The envelope is dated February 14, 1966, and in a freshly learned script it says "Daddy." In clear print above it reads: "This Is the Last Valentine I'll Ever Give You Hand to Hand. Treasure It!" The card is covered with x's and o's, and it is signed, "Love with all my might and more, Julie."

My mother went in to see my fourth-grade teacher, Mr. Birnbaum, and explained to him that she and my father were divorcing, that it might have repercussions. She asked him to be sensitive to the changes in me, to understand any erratic behavior. In school we learned about Switzerland and Jerrold Temko won the class game, the King of the Alps. I had to write a report on Ferdinand Magellan, and Jacqui and I invented complicated spy games at recess.

In March I wrote,

Dear Daddy-O,
The M in MDL stands for MUCH. The D stands

for DADDY. The L stands for Love. Altogether
I LOVE YOU MUCH DADDY!
Roses are red
Violets are blue
I Love you so much
I CAN'T EXPRESS IT TO YOU.
Love, Japanese Air Lines

Answer . . .

Dear Julie, [he wrote]
J is for the precious Jewel you are to me.
U is for the most Unusual daughter.
L is my Love for you forever.
I is for the Itch you never let me scratch.
E is for how wonderfully Easy it is to be your
   Daddy.
Love and kisses, Daddy-O

It was never that easy again.


The day my father left us, he gave me the blue and
green marble egg that had been on his dresser for
years. When he had moved out of the master bedroom
into the guest room, the egg had changed dressers too.
When he moved out of the house, the egg was mine.

It was a windy day in April, a Wednesday I remember, because I didn't go to Girl Scouts. My mother
stayed upstairs, pretending to pack winter clothes in
mothballs, and Abigail raced outside with Smokey. I

was all eyes. I watched my father tie up his boxes with string and unhook his favorite paintings, leaving white spaces on the walls. He flipped through photo albums, unsticking baby pictures of Abigail and me. He loaded his maroon Buick Skylark; the spotless black vinyl seats creased under the weight of his possessions. As he walked slowly through the house, he was so tall he had to bend down for the low doorways. I followed him into the den. He pulled one book out of the bookcase; his manicured fingers smoothed yellow pages before he replaced it. At the hall closet he took his coats, letting the hangers clang to the floor. Watching himself in the mirror, he put on one light jacket, smoothing back his black hair and focusing on the clear blue of his eyes. That was when he saw me, looking up at him with wide, dark eyes.

He was my Daddy. He was the one who watched TV with me late at night when I was supposed to be asleep; he knew I was a night owl just like him. He was the one who left notes on my pillow for me to find before I went to sleep. He was the one who rolled down the hill in the backyard with me, not even caring about the grass stains. Now, when he caught me in the mirror, he hugged me to him. I put my arms around his waist and we stood like that for a long time; I watched us in the mirror. He whispered to me that he would always be my Daddy and that no matter what he would love me. My sister burst in the room then, afraid that he would leave without saying goodbye. At the sight of her pink cheeks, tiny potbelly, and bangs, he grabbed her up and squeezed her until she cried. We three held each other, smelling the grass and his cologne, and he drew in the smell of us in his house for the last time.

My mother never came downstairs that day, and he never mentioned anything about saying good-bye to her. Right before he left he handed me the marble egg. He had known that I loved it, that I used to sneak into his room and hold its cool marble to my cheek. He kissed us each twice and got into his car. It left no tracks in the newly graveled driveway and we kept on waving long after the maroon Buick Skylark was out of sight.

# 9

Deciding upon a divorce agreement which would satisfy both my mother and my father was a difficult task. Abigail and I were immediately awarded to my mother; there had been no question about that. They argued about "visiting rights," how often we would see my father, how to divide up the summer vacation. At first my father wanted to take Abigail for one month and me for the other. My mother fought against that, because she said it was ridiculous to split us up after we had just been through one painful separation. They settled on Wednesday as the day my father would spend the afternoon and evening with us in Westport. We would take the train into New York every other weekend and go away with him for the month of August. I missed my father, so I was glad to know that there would be fixed times for me to see him. I couldn't have known then how disruptive this kind of life would be for all of us. From now on, seeing my father was to be a scheduled event. The spontaneity was gone and something very different took its place.

I looked forward to coming home from school Wednesday afternoons. A half hour after I arrived, I could hear my father's car splashing through the deep puddle in our driveway. He usually stayed outside in the car, waiting for us. I don't know if he wasn't "allowed" in or if he just didn't want to come in. All I knew was that the house he had chosen and loved was no longer his.

First we went bowling. I don't know how we picked this sport, but it was a good way for the three of us to *do* something together. The atmosphere in the bowling alley was loud and it smelled like hot dogs. I loved the whole rigmarole: the tie shoes that I wouldn't be caught dead in anywhere else, the specially marked balls (Abby liked the one with the blue star because it was the lightest), the score sheets. Was there a man back there resetting the pins, standing them up in perfect order? How did it work? I never understood.

Abby was so small she could barely lift the heavy black egg. She had to raise it slowly to her chest and push it down the alley with a shove that almost sent her sprawling. Her fingers were too short to fit in the holes which were so deep they looked like tunnels. My father loved to watch Abigail as she tilted her tiny body at the head and waist, following the movement of the ball down the aisle. She stood very still, waiting, hoping, talking to the ball as it rolled slowly down toward the pins, inching it over with her fingers in the air. Nine times out of ten it would drop into the gutter with a disappointing thud and she would turn around, her mouth in a pout.

I could lift the ball, but it landed in the gutter almost every time. I watched it start down the center and then suddenly veer to the left, as though a magnet was pulling it off course. This made me cry every week. It seemed beyond my control. My father tried to console me, saying that lefties always have it rough, that lefties have a natural curve to their throw, and maybe one day when I learned to control it, it would become an advantage. "Sure, Daddy," I would say, and watch openmouthed as he totaled his spares and strikes and walked out, a proud lefty with a 175 score. My score was almost always in the 60s, although once I hit a jackpot and got a 74. My father was proud of me then, I could tell.

After bowling, Abby and I were usually depressed, and my father would take us out to dinner to make us forget our failure as future bowling queens. La Gondolier was our spot, a "French" restaurant decorated in vinyl, not far from the bowling alley. It did not have the best food or the warmest atmosphere. We continued to go because we liked the routine. We knew the waitresses and told them what we wanted to order without even looking at the menu. My father flirted with the waitresses, trying to get them to blush. He would ask them how they were, what was new, and did they know that we were his two daughters and weren't we beautiful? Some humored him and played along, although others refused to smile.

My favorite part about La Gondolier, however, was that from the seat where I always sat, I could see everyone who entered the restaurant. I decided that I would pick my father's next bride. A 198-pound elephant would saunter down the stairs, her hair teased out six inches from her head. I would look her up and down and say, "Don't turn around, Daddy, but *she* has just walked in. She is *the* one for you. You'll love her." Abby and I would giggle in our napkins, trying to keep straight faces. By the time he turned around we could no longer hold in our laughter. He would take a look at the beauty I had picked out for him and say, "So that's who you think is right for your poor old Dad, huh?" We would continue eating until the next lovely lady entered.

We saved the best for last. After dinner, instead of ordering a stale chocolate eclair in the restaurant, we crossed the street to Carvel's. Soft, cool vanilla ice cream, dipped in chocolate, a "Brown Bonnet" they called it in ice cream lingo. Abby couldn't lick hers fast enough. Any time of year it melted, dripping down the cone, onto her fingers, and invariably onto the precious clean leather of my father's car seats. No matter how many paper napkins she wrapped around the cone, it dripped, leaked out the bottom, or fell, splat, in her lap. Out she went, banished from the crystal clean kingdom. Sometimes I joined her on the curb, trying to teach her how to lap it up around the edges while my father watched us, evening out his cone perfectly in the front seat.

She learned, eventually. By that time my father had stopped taking us out on Wednesdays. Today he says that I asked him not to come after a couple of months, but I don't remember that. All I remember is that Wednesdays became like all the other days; afternoons of homework or handball or a bike ride down Marion Road. We continued to see my father every other weekend. Bowling has never been the same. No one else understands the curve ball the losing lefty inevitably throws.

April 22, 1966

To: The Perfect Daddy
To: The Doctor
Dear Daddy,

How are you? What's new? Are you lonesome? I sent a chain letter to Barbara all the way to England. I hope she gets it.

Daddy, you said you'd write, well? If you would type it to me I would like that. YOU DO HAVE A TYPEWRITER, DON'T YOU??!! I miss you very much. I typed this letter by myself. Sorry about the mistakes.

Love,
Punkin

xxxxxxxxxxxxxxxxxxxoooooooooooooooooooooooo

My father lived in an apartment on 74th Street and Lexington Avenue. I liked the small kitchen and his room with the bed in an alcove. There was a couch that opened into a bed for Abigail and me, a long living room with low furniture and expensive paintings.

Every other Saturday morning Abigail and I rushed around our house looking for socks and nightgowns, hairbrushes and toothpaste. We were preparing for the weekend with Daddy. No matter what time we woke up we were never ready when my mother yelled for us to get into the car to go to the station. Saturday mornings were times for fights.

"Julie, hurry up, we're going to miss the train!"

"Mommy, I can't find my other shoe!" I would whine.

"Look under the bed. Abby, where is your brush? You look like you haven't combed your hair in weeks."

"Mommy, I tried to find it for her. I looked everywhere."

"I lost it," Abby would say, sitting in front of the television watching cartoons, her legs folded out behind her in a position no one else could figure out.

"Julie, is your suitcase packed?"

"Yeah, but I don't have any room for my book."

"Carry it. Oh, let's go!" my mother would say, thoroughly exasperated.

In the beginning we'd get dressed up to go see my father. We wore sleeveless dresses and ankle socks; Abby wore her Mary-Janes and I had matured into flat black shoes. We kept the hair out of our eyes with elastic hairbands, and I carried a purse, a carryover from my elegant days at the beach. I had dispensed with the white gloves and fan because they became too dirty on the train.

It was a big decision for my mother to let us take

the train by ourselves. She knew my father was meeting us at the other end, so she allowed us to go. She bought our tickets and we boarded the train, our little suitcases bulging with too many pairs of underpants and holey undershirts. We waved good-bye while the train pulled out and her figure became smaller until all we could see was the movement of her hand. I could never tell if she had been crying behind her glasses.

For Abby and me, the hour ride to New York was a very long trip. Sometimes my mother bought us magazines and we read them; other times we brought a pad and two pens and played ticktacktoe and hangman. But our problem was solved when we started looking out the window for a stretch of fifteen miles. We made an astonishing discovery: almost every house we could see from Norwalk through Stamford had a small, round, built-aboveground swimming pool in its backyard. There was no question in our minds: this was Pool Country, the strange land where inexpensive home-built swimming pools were taking the place of swing sets and sandboxes. We began counting them as quickly as we could. Usually we reached thirty when we lost track and realized we had missed those two in the corner or the three hidden by the trees. There were never people swimming in the pools, just light blue circles of still water. They looked like rings in the circus, illuminated by giant spotlights.

After passing through Pool Country, Abby and I

made up a new game. One time one of us had been crying. Either there had been a fight with our mother, or we were missing our best friend's birthday party and didn't really want to go to New York. I took a tear on the tip of my finger and Abby and I discussed every possibility of where this tear could go. It traveled first down her cheek and off onto her dress, down her legs and into her shoes. Or it made its way onto the seat and floated down to the fingernail of the ninety-year-old lady in the last seat of the furthest car. This tear reappeared every other Saturday morning; its adventures helped to pass the time.

We also played I Spy, a game where one of us picked an object and described it only by its color. The other person had to guess what the object was. These games occupied us for most of the time, but the hour and eleven minutes still dragged.

Stepping off the train and walking up the long path to the gate was my favorite part. My father was always the tallest person waiting; we could spot him immediately. It was very comforting to know he was there. I didn't have to be in charge of my little sister anymore. He would take our suitcases and kiss us each twice. Sometimes he brought his car and we would drive up to his apartment.

This was new for all of us. We were a new kind of abbreviated family. We would sit in the kitchen and talk. From time to time my father brushed the hair out of my eyes and put it behind my ears. He would smooth my temples with the palm of his hand. The three of us went shopping together. Abby had become a picky eater and didn't like anything. She wouldn't eat jelly on her toast or ketchup on her hamburgers. She hated all vegetables and sauces. The one thing my father bought that we all loved was a coffee milkshake in a can. He would lift the can high and scoop it up and down as he poured it, always landing the thick liquid right in the glass. We tried to imitate him and it spilled all over the kitchen table.

Steven and David came over some Saturdays and we watched TV or went to the movies. My father wouldn't let them see my mother anymore, so they never came up to Westport. My mother was very upset about that. She never forgave him for it.

Sometimes we visited Grandma Sallie; other times we took a bus to the zoo. We would go for long walks in Central Park and sit around the pool where Stuart Little had had his sailboat race. My father would buy us ice cream cones and hot dogs and we would watch the people bicycle by.

Sundays we tried to recapture our family Sundays in Westport. My father would play Brandenburg concertos and we would read the funnies. Later we would go out to dinner and David would always order the most expensive thing on the menu.

A couple of weekends my father took the four of us to visit his sister in Connecticut. Abby and I wore pink snowsuit jackets and loafers. We made paths around the empty pool in winter, crunching dry leaves under our feet. There is a picture of my father and us taken on one of those visits. We are all holding on to one part of him and he has his arms around us, pulling us closer.

My father grew his hair long and listened to The

Mamas and The Papas. He refused to look older. He stopped wearing ties and took to sporting a beret. He asked us about our mother, as though we were the keepers of all her secrets.

"Is your mother still seeing that artist?" he would say, trying to act as though he didn't care one way or the other.

"Yeah, I guess so," I would say. I didn't like to talk to him about my mother. I felt I had to defend her.

"Does she say that they're going to get married?"

"No. She doesn't say anything."

"Does he live there?" looking at me, hard.

"No, Daddy. Let's go watch TV," I'd say. Abby bit her nails.

My father bought us new corduroy suitcases so that when we came to see him we would look respectable. We always got the feeling that we were never quite clean enough, that there were too many creases in our clothes. This, of course, was another way for him to find fault with our mother. He blamed Abby's eating habits on our grandfather and our mother.

"Abigail, when are you going to eat right? Not only do you eat with your fingers, but you're just like your mother's father. He likes everything burned and plain. And your mother has always hated tomatoes."

"Mommy *loves* tomatoes," I'd say. "It's just us who hate them."

"Your mother never ate a tomato in front of me."

"Well, Daddy, people change." By then I would be on the verge of tears.

I was very protective of my sister. I believed that she was afraid of my father and couldn't defend herself. I was afraid of him too, sometimes, because his angry voice seemed all-powerful. He was so tall and knowing that it was difficult for me to contradict him. I still loved him, even when he hurt me or insulted my mother. But he could make me cry as no one else could. He knew he had this power over me.

The weekends were fun, but there was a difference between the life we lived at home and the time we spent with our father. Nothing that we did there with him corresponded to our everyday lives. My father didn't really know who my friends were or what I was learning at shcool. He didn't know how intensely I lived my friendships, how I loved beating the boys at handball. I showed him my report cards, but he was no longer a part of the process. I did my math homework on my own; I studied for tests and won the fourth-grade spelling bee without his being aware of it. Our lives were linked, by blood, by love, by weekends in New York. But he did not watch Abby and me grow up daily. Our visits were tinged with sadness.

The weekends went by very quickly. Before he started going out with other women, there was no one else to visit. Before taking the 6:05 home on Sunday nights, I expected to go to the Hickory Pit, a restaurant where I could get my ideal dinner for $1.39. I always ordered a steak the shape of Fire Island which was so thin even Abby could cut it without help. He offered to take us to a real restaurant, but at the age of 9½ I enjoyed being a regular there.

The gray-haired waiter winked at me those Sundays. He kept a chewed pencil behind his ear.

We spent so much time at Grand Central Station that it was like a home to Abby and me. We knew the high ceilings which arched above us farther than the sky in the Hayden Planetarium and the big clock which always reminded us how little time there was to catch our train. Color Kodak ads stretched across an entire wall; the people in them were *too* happy, *too* earnest, *too* American. We avoided the old women who shuffled around in bare feet, talking to their shopping bags. Abby and I walked quickly and looked no one in the eye, our corduroy suitcases banging against our short legs.

As we got on the train with our father, we saw other fathers sending their kids home to Mommy, too.

We came to know these trains very well: the old ones, with blue plush seats stained and worn from so much sitting, the stairs you had to climb to reach the car. There was no intercom in those days, just a conductor who strode down the aisle like the town crier, announcing the stops. And there was the candy man, who slid onto the train ten minutes before it was supposed to leave, carrying a case full of Baby Ruth and Heath bars, licorice and "cold drinks"— cartons of sugary orange juice which were always lukewarm. As the conductor shouted "All aboard!" he quickly made change and disappeared off the train.

It was a weekend ritual, a new way to keep a broken

family whole. The fathers had an unspoken bond. They looked guiltily at each other, kissing their children good-bye extra hard, and slipped them dollar bills in case of emergency. And we, the brave travelers, settled back in our seats to go home. We waved good-bye to Daddy, who made faces at us through the window. His monkey faces embarrassed us, but we loved them anyway. We giggled and motioned for him to leave, but when he did there was no one. The train would start with a jolt, and Daddy, New York, and artificial coffee milkshakes disappeared for another long two weeks. We were his two little girls; he had the rest of Sunday night ahead of him, alone.

Returning to Westport after weekends with Daddy was another adjustment. Our mother picked us up at the station and informed us as to who had called, what we had missed. On Sunday nights my mother either wore her long Mexican dress or old pants. She had spent the hour before preparing us dinner, a feat for her. We opened the back door to the smell of chicken cacciatore. Smokey was thrilled at our return and licked our cheeks and mouths.

My mother seemed sad those Sundays. I could tell she was glad that we were home, but the weekend without us had left its mark. She tried to sound cheerful and curious, and she never once said that she had been lonely. But Sundays were family days, and when we weren't there it just wasn't the same. Our Sundays with her were filled with classical music and the *New*

*York Times*, the comics, a big breakfast and being cozy all day. For my friends, Sunday was the day that their fathers were home from work. They had early afternoon suppers and TV together at night. We had our own routine, our own Sunday dinner at the Artists' Pub, a small restaurant at the bottom of the hill. Or we went to Carroll's and had 43¢ hamburgers. During our weekends with my father, my mother occupied herself with her friends and her work. We were her family and we weren't there. Abby and I felt sorry for her, even though she told us not to worry.

There was a final part to this weekend ritual which didn't please any of us. Going upstairs to unpack our suitcases, Abby and I were occasionally horrified at the sight of one of our pets floating on its side in the fish tank or sitting motionless like a rock underwater. We had fish, parakeets, turtles, and hamsters over the course of the next few years, and one of them always chose the weekends we were away to die. Often my mother forgot to feed them, but sometimes they just died. After being away it was very frightening and sad to return to my room and find a dead animal there. I always made my mother bury them, for I was afraid to touch anything dead. She told us she dug holes for them in the backyard, but I'm sure many fish were flushed down the toilet when Abby and I weren't looking.

My mother asked us how we spent our weekends with our father.

"Didn't he take you to any museums or anything?"

"No, Ma. He just likes to *be* with us. We don't have to *do* things," I would say.

"But New York is such a wonderful city. There is so much he could do with you and still just be with you if he used a little imagination."

"We went to see the girls who live next door to Grandma Sallie," Abby said. "We played cards."

"Now that's exciting," my mother would say, unconvinced.

My father rarely called us during the week just to talk or "shoot the breeze." We wrote a few letters back and forth, but the only times he would call were to make arrangements for meeting us at the train. He didn't believe in small talk, he said, or calling for the sake of calling. My mother criticized him for that, but I didn't know what else to expect and I didn't complain. If he did call and my mother answered the phone, we knew immediately that it was he. Her voice changed, her attitude became superior, and she was on the battlefield once more. Usually she gave the phone to me, but sometimes they had a good fight first. No matter how much time had passed between their calls or chance meetings, her anger would surface quickly.

It was during this period that I began keeping a journal, a habit that I have continued to this day. May 25, 1966, was my first entry. One Wednesday after my father had spent the day with us, I wrote in my journal, "Mommy and Daddy had a fight today. Boy was it loud. I wish they were married. SOB!

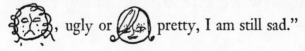, ugly or pretty, I am still sad."

# 10

The first summer after the divorce my mother rented our house to a young couple from New York. In June, we moved to my grandparents' house in Weston. It was odd leaving our home, packing valuables away in closets, and stripping the beds. My mother needed the money, she said, and we could live at Grandma's free.

I brought with me a framed picture of my mother and father when they were first married. No one understood why I liked this picture because my mother had short, curly red hair, the result of one afternoon's whim at the beauty parlor. Her smile is young and even, and a string of pearls curls around her throat. My father smiles so broadly there is a glimmer of the gold from his back teeth. They are happy and appear at ease with each other. It was the only picture

I had of them together. I still liked it, even though it was no longer true. It didn't make sense anymore, but I held on to it, as I held on to my love for my father and my memories of him in our house.

In July, Abby and I went to day camp. The three of us slept in the cottage next to the big house. Abby and I had a small room with two beds and a dresser with lamps shaped like ducks.

In the mornings before camp we would eat our Cinnamon Pop-Tarts and watch the Little Rascals and Donna Reed on TV. We made up games as we waited at the bus stop, holding our bag lunches of peanut butter (hers) and jelly (mine) sandwiches, Fritos, and Devil Dogs. At camp I performed as Peter Pan in a play and we both won All-Around Camper awards.

We talked to our father on the phone from time to time, and in August he rented a house in Ocean Beach, Fire Island. I hadn't been there since my drooling days, and I was excited to return to a place where, as a baby, I had learned to walk in the sand.

Abigail and I said good-bye to our mother and promised to write long, detailed letters. My father drove us out to the ferry and we crossed the bay to Fire Island. Grandma Sallie came too, and over the next week or so, David and Steven arrived. It was the first time we were to spend more than a weekend with my father. We would wake up and see him in his bathrobe again, eat cinnamon toast in the morning with him, and spend the day happy just knowing that he was around. All of the things that other children considered very normal, a way of life I had once taken for granted, was suddenly a new adjustment for me to make.

Our room had low ceilings and green bedspreads, and at night the mosquitoes buzzed around our ears until we thought we'd go crazy. The first night Abigail wet her bed and was very embarrassed in the morning. I told her not to worry, that that happened all the time when you're in a new place. She didn't want me to tell our father, but I knew she needed clean sheets and I didn't know where to get them. I told Grandma Sallie, and she helped us remake the bed.

I had just cut my hair to my shoulders and was feeling older. I was happy to be with my father, although his constant teasing made me cry, his drawing attention to the changes in me embarrassed me. One of the first days I was there, I came downstairs in my one-piece bathing suit. My 9½-year-old flat chest was just beginning to grow; two tiny buds had appeared. Because there were long periods of time between my visits with my father, my development had not been gradual for him, but very sudden. To him it seemed as though I were changing too quickly.

"What have you got there?" he said, pointing at my chest with his finger. He was smiling; he thought that I would too and we both would have a good laugh about it. I was horrified. He had brought attention to my most vulnerable spot. I burst into tears and ran up to my room, refusing to come out. Everyone went to the beach while I stayed there reading. Later that day, Grandma Sallie came up and told me that my

father had just been teasing and that it wasn't anything
to lose sleep over. I hadn't lost any sleep and I didn't
exactly understand what she meant, but I was hungry
and wanted to come down by then anyway. Something changed between my father and me that day. I
was growing up and we didn't know what to do about
it. That was one of the times I missed my mother and
wished I were home.

It was the summer I discovered chocolate chip mint
ice cream and saw *The Yellow Submarine* with my
brothers. It was hearing the Beatles' *Revolver* album
blasted onto our street at all hours of the day. David
and Steven were at the "cool" age and they experimented with new things and loud music. They made
friends at the beach; Abby and I just had each other.

We were still getting used to this new way of life
when my father introduced us to Vivian. Vivian was
a young Italian woman with full breasts and very red
lips. She was dark and tanned beautifully. She made
me feel small and imperfect. First she came to the
beach with us, but then she began staying over in the
extra room downstairs. I remember watching her
comb out her hair after her shower, putting on her
makeup much more delicately than my mother did.
My father was not reserved around her. I saw him kiss
her good morning in the same way he had kissed my
mother once. I believe my father was quite taken with
her until she started talking too much about her
personal problems.

After a while Vivian disappeared and my father
met another woman on the beach. Her name was
Judy and she wore her hair in pigtails. She had two

small children and a large cesarean scar on her brown
stomach. She was Jewish and divorced and easy to get
along with. Abby and I liked her and her kids and
we didn't mind spending several evenings at their
house.

My father always needed someone. He had to have
someone to dazzle, to tease, to love. We had a good
time that summer, but it didn't feel like a family.
These other women weren't my mother, and my
father was constantly in pursuit of a relationship,
grounded only by us. The last week we were there
my mother sent me the letter from school saying who
my fifth-grade teacher was to be. Normally she would
have called with information like that, but my father
didn't like her to call when we were with him. He
didn't like us to be in two places at once, he said.
"Mr. Gee," it read, and I thought, *A Chinese man for
a fifth-grade teacher?* I knew the summer was almost
over. I began thinking about my real life again, my
day-to-day routine, my mother and friends, Smokey
and the hamsters. It was time to go home.

When we moved back into our house in September,
the guest room had been made over into my room.
The double bed had a laced-together bamboo back-
board, and my mother and the artist she was seeing,
Michael, had attached all of my stuffed animals onto
it. It no longer resembled my father's "interim" room.
Abigail was moved into Steven's and David's room. It
was as if we were starting all over.

Every night when I got into bed, I would pretend

I was the teacher of a class and take out my three-ring binder entitled "Play School." I would talk out loud to my "students," of whom Hannah and Emily were my favorites. I loved being at the other end of the classroom and being *all* of the students at the same time. I corrected their papers and encouraged them in their rehearsals of *Fiddler on the Roof*. Then I would fill my journal with the events of both "Play School" and my real life. I was thrilled that no one knew about my moonlighting as a teacher at night.

The first Christmas without my father, my mother came down with a mysterious disease called labyrinthitis. She was so dizzy she couldn't walk, and every time she tried to stand up she thought she would faint. Luckily she had bought many of our Christmas presents already; Abby and I knew because when she was at work we would find the key to the closet and sneak a look at what was inside. That year we only had the chance to see my sleeping bag and some books before my mother got sick and stayed in her room all the time. One Christmas not long after, we opened every box prematurely, then cleverly rewrapped everything exactly the way it had been. On Christmas morning we tried to look surprised, even though we had had time to prepare our reactions.

My mother took great pride in giving us lots of presents on Christmas, although she didn't really believe in it and would much rather have celebrated Chanukah with one present a night for eight days. This Chanukah we brought the menorah up to her room. By the eighth night she managed to sit up and say the prayers with us. We turned out the lights. Our

faces were solemn as Abby lit the candles. The menorah was a music box and we hummed along with its
tinny "Rock of Ages." Only Abby knew the words.

It wasn't until Christmas day that my father's absence was painfully obvious. However, Abby and I
were still excited on the early winter morning. It had
snowed the night before and our house settled beautifully into the cushion of the white ground. We tried
to awaken our mother at six, but decided to be lenient
with her because she had been sick.

The presents were hastily wrapped; the ones she
had bought at the last minute were in newspaper. It
was a smaller Christmas, we could see that. My mother
had warned us, saying that she really didn't have that
much money. But she had tried to make the room look
fuller with a lot of green leaves and branches—her
concession to a tree. She had stuffed our stockings
with walnuts and lollipops; they looked like snakes
swallowing little round animals whole. It took much
longer to get my mother downstairs when she was
alone, and she had trained me how to make her coffee
so that it would be perking when she arrived in the
kitchen. Her entrance signified the beginning. Abby
sat on her chair and I kneeled on the floor and we
slowly, lovingly, opened our presents.

My father made a big fuss about seeing us on holidays. He insisted that we spend Christmas day with
him, even if that meant we had to take the train into
New York. On holidays he asserted his rights as half
owner of the property which was my sister and me.
On Christmas I was always the one to have tearful

telephone conversations with my father. Of course we wanted to be with him, I'd say, but we didn't want to leave our mother alone in our big house, and besides, our grandparents were coming over for dinner. If we suggested the day after Christmas or even the next weekend, he was furious and mumbled that he hated being in competition with my grandparents. He made me feel extremely guilty, as though it were my fault that my parents didn't live together and I still had loyal feelings for both.

I had sent him two Christmas cards which I hoped would make up for my absence. One was signed, "Love and smoochaberries, Pungin (don't forget the G)." The other was a card I had made myself. On the cover it said, "To the best Daddy in the world." I wanted him to know that I missed him. That year we went into New York the day after Christmas, and my father invited his new girl friend, Mary, to celebrate with us.

Mary was in the cosmetic business and she looked like an Avon lady. She was blond and her skin glowed without any imperfections. My father had been seeing her for a while, judging by his familiarity with her. To my surprise, after my father had given us his presents, we took a cab to Mary's apartment and she brought out a small bag full of perfectly wrapped, delicately scented gifts. In my journal I wrote,

From Mary:   1. ribbons
             2. cologne and bath powder
             3. mirror.

I didn't know if this was her way of making a comment about my appearance or if she was trying to make me feel older, or if these were the only free gifts she could get. I took them home on the train and added them to my collection.

Among all my friends, I was the only one who celebrated two Christmases. And from now on, it was to be two birthdays, two Thanksgivings, and two Passovers. Family days were difficult times because I wanted to be with both of my parents and couldn't. I usually ended up crying and feeling guilty no matter what my decision. My father didn't help because he expected us to be with him, regardless of anyone else's plans. It became a kind of tug-of-war, and Abby and I slid from side to side, never quite sure what was the right thing to do. As the years went on my father had a tougher battle to fight, for Westport became more and more our *home*. He was on the outside, a voice on the telephone, speaking to me with hurt pride and thinly veiled resentment.

January 20, 1967
Today is Gay's birthday party. I can't go because we're going to New York. RATS!

January 21, 1967
We are in New York with Daddy. I love him!

January 22, 1967
Today is Abigail's birthday. We visited Gloria, Daddy's girl friend. Her daughters Kelly, 10, and

Amy, 5, are nice. I hope Daddy marries her. I might get jealous though. I wonder why Gloria didn't kiss me good-bye. I wish she had. P.S. I got a 103 on my arithmetic test. One hundred and <u>three</u>!

My father didn't like to be alone. He wasn't indiscriminate in whom he spent his time with, but it seemed that *anyone* was preferable to solitude. At the time I just tried to keep up with him and his "girl friends." I was shy and quiet until I knew them well. And by that time he was ready to move on to the next. In some ways I knew that it was right for my father to be going out a lot, yet it still felt strange to see him kiss other women. My mother continued seeing Michael in Westport. For the most part, he was a constant in our lives, although she did go out with other men. Whenever Abby and I knew a man was coming to pick up our mother, we would hide upstairs and refuse to answer the doorbell. This infuriated her, for she was never ready when her date arrived. With one eye made up, she would run down, show him into the living room, and run back up into her bathroom, grimacing at us on the way. Sometimes we sat at the top of the stairs, hoping for a peek at him, and other times she made us come down and shake hands. There weren't that many of them, and they were always very smiley and eager to ask us questions. We knew that none of these men really meant much to our mother.

My father believed in introducing us immediately

and thoroughly to his current girl friends. So it was that our weekends with Daddy inevitably ended up being weekends with Daddy and ——. We met Gloria, her two daughters, and their dog, Samantha, soon after my father did. She lived in Westport too, in a dark gray house at the top of a hill. They lived in a different section of town, so we had never crossed paths. Steven and David came with us to see her and the six of us kids went bike riding.

Gloria had large blue eyes and small smooth lips. Her hands were graceful and her ears well shaped and delicate. I thought she was beautiful, and I could tell my father did, too. Kelly was my age and I slept in the same room with her. She had a brass bed and pictures of horses all over her room. Amy was blond and all arms and legs. She was only five but seemed much younger than Abby at six. Kelly and Amy visited their father on the same weekends we stayed with our mother, so that every time we came to Gloria's they were there with us.

The next year was a confusing one for me. I was in fifth grade and very concerned with friends and grades. My teacher, Mr. Gee, turned out *not* to be Chinese, but a twenty-two-year-old man just out of college. I had a crush on him and hated him at the same time. He attached a miniature basketball hoop to the garbage can in our classroom and he and the boys tried to make baskets with crumpled-up arithmetic tests. He loved teasing me, calling me nicknames, and writing funny comments on my papers. One day I wore my hair in two bunches and he dubbed me "Pigtails" from then on. Another day he asked to see a linoleum print I had made. I thought it was so awful I refused. He badgered me, saying that he'd give me an F in his grade book unless I showed him. I held fast and when he proudly displayed the red F next to my name, I started to cry.

My mother hated the winter and the cold. She began to be disenchanted with our old house, even though she knew it was special. "It's too big for us now," she told me. "I can't afford it and we need something smaller." I was horrified. I loved our house almost as much as I loved my mother and father. It *was* my mother and father, for me. At first she hadn't wanted to move because she said there had been enough disruption in our lives for a while. Originally she insisted on staying in the house because it was familiar; it was home, even though my father's absence was painfully noticeable. In February she began looking at other houses with real estate agents, and families were herded around our rooms like tourists.

"Oh, Henry, don't you think our chartreuse chaise longue would look wonderful there?" I'd hear. "Sylvia, your vanity would fit right in that corner beneath the mirror." I would leave the house when these people came because I didn't like them walking on *my* floors, touching *my* furniture. I became very possessive of that house and everything in it.

My mother found a little brown house not far from ours for us to rent. She brought Abby and me over and we timidly climbed the stairs, clutching the banisters. We were excited by the thought of something new, but terrified of losing our home.

Just as she was about to sign the lease, my mother

changed her mind. We were relieved. She decided to rent our house for the summers instead. We hated that, too, but it was better than leaving it forever.


That year we spent Saturdays in New York with our father and Sundays with Gloria in Westport. Sometimes we stayed at Gloria's for the entire weekend. It was strange to be in the same town we lived in but not to be with our mother. We made the transition after a while.

My diary is full of my grades, my friends, movies and plays I had seen. The memo from February, 1967, reads:

Daddy loves Kelly and Amy and Gloria. I'm jealous. I try not to show it but it's hard.

March 12, 1967
Mom thinks I don't mind about Dad and Gloria! She thinks I'm happy! I'm not always.


The winter of 1967 there were blizzards every day for weeks at a time, and occasionally school was canceled. When the spring started to break through, my mother's winter depression lifted. We celebrated the sharp purple points of the first crocus's arrival.

My father bought cameras for both Abby and me, and the first weekend in April he took us, Gloria, Kelly, and Amy to Sherwood Island to take pictures. The beach was still chilly and deserted so early in the spring, and we wore heavy sweaters. There are photographs from that day of Gloria holding Kelly close to her, of Amy down by the water, Abby sitting on a boulder, my father and Gloria, their faces next to each other. We all snapped pictures of each other taking pictures, our hair blowing in our faces. Abby looks very small, her baggy Danskin pants bunching around her knees. I am wearing the striped sweater my father gave me for Christmas. Kelly and I are about the same height, but I remember feeling much bigger. It was our first family outing.

The only times I saw Steven and David were the weekends with my father and Gloria. It was a situation we were all thrown into, and we weren't entirely comfortable with it, yet we knew there was nothing we could do about it. Those Saturdays at 74th Street were over, and the feeling that my father was a lonely divorcé had disappeared. I knew I was losing something, and even then I was aware of my own jealousy. I was afraid that Steven and David preferred having Kelly and Amy as their sisters to Abigail and me. And, as I wrote in my diary on April 16, "Daddy took us this weekend. I think sometimes he loves Gloria more than me! Probably not!"

# 11

Sometime in the next six months, my father told us that he and Gloria were getting married. I don't recall how I felt when he told me. It is one of those instances which I have blocked from my memory. However, I remember in detail the day of my father's wedding in 1967, a year after my father and Gloria had met.

Abigail and I spent a long time dressing that morning. We could not decide what to wear. I was eleven and Abby was seven and the fact that our father was *really* getting married again caught us unaware. We could not buckle our shoes or button our dresses in the right way; our fingers were cold and shook slightly. I thought I should dress in bright colors, but under the circumstances, even though I didn't do it, it seemed more appropriate to wear black.

It was a clear, cold day in December and the ground

was covered with a fine snow. When our father came
to pick us up to go to the Unitarian church, we stepped
shyly out into the driveway, our feet in black patent
leather shoes, our winter coats identical. His feet made
large firm prints; ours were small and tentative. He
and Gloria were coiffed, perfumed, and ready, and
they were no less talkative than usual. My father
smoked and blew rings for us, our favorite trick of his.
Gloria looked into the mirror repeatedly, wetting and
smoothing her eyebrows, her cat eyes sharp in the
reflection. She didn't know that we were watching
her.

Once inside the church, a wooden arklike building
full of windows, Abigail and I sat in the front row next
to Grandma Sallie. Her hair was piled up in a bun on
her head and her purse matched her dress. She slipped
us mint Life Savers and warmed our cold hands in both
of hers. Steven and David sat behind us in ties and
polished loafers. Their faces hid more than ours did;
they were old hands at this. They even laughed at
each other's jokes. Abigail and I giggled uneasily. We
turned around in our seats and watched the church fill
up. The people entered two by two and sat in couples.
The ceiling seemed very high, the glass in the windows
hazy; the thin branches outside shivered in the wind.

Suddenly all was quiet and the music began. My
father and Gloria moved down the aisle toward us.
Their friends nodded at the couple's beauty, at the
harmony of their footsteps. My father seemed very
tall and his lips were set in a new determination: this
marriage would work. Gloria looked like an Indian

princess. She wore bright beads and her nose was straight and proud. Their hands were clasped and even their breathing seemed on the same beat. As they approached their heels clicked louder and louder until they reached the front.

The ceremony was short. I neither saw nor heard it. I was very small, a pinpoint, and I sat quite still, holding Abigail's nailbitten hand. In the instant of their kiss, I knew it was sealed. They turned to come back up the aisle, smiling relief and renewal. I could no longer maintain the position of my face. It slipped away from me. My lips twisted and I cried for the finality of that moment, definite and irreversible. He really wasn't coming home anymore: no more television alone together, no more watching him shave in front of the mirror, no more hot chocolate on Sunday mornings, no more foursome, no more family, no more Daddy. He would live in a new house and buy new slippers, watch television with Gloria's daughters, and see us only on weekends. We would be weekend children forever, reserved like rental books in the library. He would check us out on Saturday morning and return us undamaged on Sunday night. We would yellow with age.

Steven hugged me and I hid my face in his jacket, in his male smell. I couldn't catch my breath and I knew people were looking at me, at my red eyes. Abigail was frightened; she clung to Grandma Sallie's skirt. When my father rejoined us I tried to smile. "It will take time," his best man said to him, standing far above me.

At the reception I wandered from room to room, feeling my dress was too short, my legs too fat. There was a wedding cake and champagne, loud music and dancing. The guests kept patting my father on the back: better luck this time! try again!

He looked taller to me that night. I wouldn't dance with him so he lifted Abigail up and spun her around. Her underwear showed under her dress; she cried and he put her down, confused.

The reception lasted until the sky was dark. No stars came out that night and the bare trees were menacing. My father and his wife drove us home. He dropped us off at the doorstep and left us with our mother. His good-bye kiss smelled of Gloria's perfume.

My journal reads simply: "December 17, 1967— Dad and Gloria got married. I knew they would all along."

I had never been good at adjusting to change. Now there was no way to postpone the changes that were to take place in my life. My father slowly began to lose the central position of importance he had held in my eyes. Energy and conflict centered around my mother and her participation in the rest of my childhood. Suddenly it was very clear that my family was the three of us: my mother, my sister, and me. I ached for the feeling of *family*, to be complete and experience a fullness which a three-person family cannot have.

We were to build a strong and impenetrable triangle

over the next six years. This triangle became the springboard from which I built my life; my father was on the outside. He could sense this happening, I am sure, although none of us could talk about it. Bit by bit his life pulled away from ours, and he placed the burden of holding our relationship together on us.

One day I wrote out a list of our entire enlarged family. I listed each member, starting with my father down to Amy, who was the youngest. I included our full names, present age, birthdate, hair color, eye color, and the hand we wrote with. My father and I were the only lefties, so I felt special. At the bottom of the long sheet of paper I wrote, "The above make up the eight people in the present List family." My mother was not mentioned, of course, because she was not part of *this* new family. Abigail and I had two families, one little and one big. We bounced back and forth between them.

That Christmas Abigail and I woke up at home and then spent the rest of the day with my father and his new family at some friends of Gloria's who lived in Westport. After the New Year they moved into a brownstone on the Upper East Side of New York. The apartment walls were covered in corduroy, and in Kelly's and Amy's room upstairs, there were two sets of bunk beds. Abigail and I had a short reprieve from the fold-out couch. They settled into New York with a bit of difficulty at first, changing schools, making new friends, learning how to walk the dog and bring keys everywhere. Even their cat had to learn to use the litter box in New York, instead of sitting on the toilet as he had been accustomed to in Westport. Their cat was the only one I had ever seen do that, and my father was determined to break him of the habit.

Although at the time I would have had a hard time explaining it, I knew there was some kind of injustice going on. *My* father was living with someone else's daughters who were almost exactly our ages and watching *them* grow up instead of us. It wasn't that I didn't like Kelly and Amy (for I really did). Kelly and I became friends slowly, as we learned to share things and talk to each other honestly. As New York began to polish her, I felt more at a distance; I felt bigger and not as well-dressed. Amy was a sensitive little girl, enjoying the role of the baby in the family. Abigail, even though she was only a year older, was too old to be Amy's equal. Abigail was always in between the ages of all of us, for she was very mature in some ways and, when we allowed her to be, a little girl in others.

Kelly and Amy loved their own father, too. He gave them expensive presents and took them riding in exotic places. He remarried a twenty-five-year-old model and Kelly and Amy spent their "other weekends" with them. The "ex-husband" received the same treatment as our mother, the "ex-wife." These cast-offs were easily maligned in their absence, while we, the intermediaries, were left to defend them.

There were bright dried flowers in the kitchen and a

bird in a white hanging cage. Pots and colanders dangled from a rack in the center of the ceiling, and some Sunday nights Gloria made us all a spaghetti dinner before we took the train back to Westport. My father seemed happy with her in those days. I loved her laugh. She tried to make Abigail and me part of their lives, but the transition was not smooth. She had had two children, and now she had six.

I got a kick out of being in such a large family. I was the eldest of two children at home, and now I was the third eldest of six. Kelly, Steven, David, and I made up the older set: we played backgammon and bought all the new records, like *Abbey Road* and Led Zeppelin, to listen to on my father's classy stereo. We did our homework together and stayed up watching "Mannix" and "Saturday Night at the Movies" long after everyone else had gone to sleep.

January 13, 1968
Today is Saturday. We are at Gloria's and Dad's. It's fun but Gloria is mean sometimes. G and D are going out tonight and so Kelly, Amy, Abigail, and I have a baby-sitter. Her name is Ray. She is from London, England. She is sort of nice. P.S. Dad luvs me more than Kelly and Amy I think.

My father accused me of being a "sourpuss," of never smiling. He said I was too serious. He tried to tease me into relaxing. Over the course of the year it became more difficult to make the transition from weekday life to weekend life. On the weekends we went to the Hayden Planetarium and I sat in silence as the black dome above us filled with stars and constellations. We leaned our heads back in our chairs and listened to the deep voice boom in the darkness. It was a comforting stillness, knowing that we were protected by the surrounding night, that we could not go anywhere. We all visited Grandma Sallie from time to time. It bothered me the way Gloria called her "Mother." Once we walked around the Museum of Natural History, several times we went to the park, but most other days we stayed home and watched TV.

February 23, 1968
Today me and Abby were watching "Dark Shadows." Right in the best part we had to go to the station to go to New York. That made me SO MAD! Now I am in New York. In my bed, writing to you. They finally have put lights in over our beds. Kelly isn't here. I am lonely without her.

Me and Dad and Steven played Monopoly. Steven lost, then me. Dad won!!! With about 50,000 dollars too!

Throughout the next six months my journal was filled with my ambivalences about living a "double life."

March 22, 1968
Tomorrow we are going to New York. I don't really want to go but . . .

March 24, 1968
New York was fun. I like it. I might be able to
bring Sally once. I hope so.

April 21, 1968
Hi. It was a great weekend. Saturday, Dad,
Abby, and I went rowing. Sunday Sally, Dad,
Gloria, Abigail, and I went bicycling. Oops!
That was today.

Sundays we slept late. In our nightgowns Kelly and
I would go downstairs and prepare our breakfast:
orange juice, frozen French toast or waffles, and
heated syrup. We knew how to make real French
toast, and if we waited long enough Gloria would
eventually come down and make it for us, but we had
fun popping our breakfast in a toaster. Amy and
Abigail would wander down, Amy still with sleep in
her eyes, Abigail in a nightgown she had outgrown
a year before. Kelly was happy that Amy had someone to play with. She considered Amy spoiled and
felt she had always gotten her way.

For me these weekends were like taking a vacation
from my real life. At home I became intensely involved in my friendships: the wavering affections of
Lise and Jacqui, Jen and Sally, were the most important concerns I had. Grades mattered a lot, and my
first crush on a boy occupied my thoughts most of
the time. I began to be aware of my depression. I
didn't know how to define it then, but it was a new,
dragging sensation which I alluded to several times in

my journal. I knew that my life was unclear and different from my friends' lives.

February 5, 1968
I don't know why, but I feel depressed. Well, good night.

February 8, 1968
I hate Richard, Mr. Gee, and Carol the most of all. I like Lise, Sally, Jen, Marisol, Diane, Cindy, Jacqui, Amy, Rory. I think that's all. I have felt depressed since the beginning of February. I can't express it. I love Mom.

March 10, 1968
Even though Mom came home (from France) I feel depressed. . . . Today I went to New York. To Dad's and we drove to 1st Street and then to the Madison Delicatessen. Good . . . I feel terrible and depressed. Well . . . good night.

March 17, 1968
Mom changed her mind again. She said at the end of the school year we might have to move! I don't want to! Oh God, please tell her not to make us. My eyes are red from crying so much. Well, good night.

March 25, 1968
Mom is so stupid. I hate her. Anything I say, "Stop being fresh, Julie." I wish I could run away. For my punishment I have to just sit and do nothing all day. . . . I wish she was nice.

April 9, 1968
I don't feel like writing. Ick. I probably won't go
to camp . . . Mom is so old and not-understand-
ing. I don't hate her but I don't luv her.

Once I actually did run away. I packed a little bag
and slammed the door behind me. About halfway out
the driveway I decided to hide in the woodpile on the
back porch instead. I knew my mother was worried
because I heard the front door open every few
minutes and she called my name into the darkness.
Once she even started the motor of her car, but I
guess she thought better of it because she never left
the house. After an hour or so I was cold and hungry
(I had missed dinner) so I nonchalantly strolled in
the back door. My mother just as nonchalantly asked,
"You want some lamb chops?"

# 12

That summer Abby and I spent the month of July with the new List family. Kelly and I took the bus to the YWCA in the East Fifties, renting the red or blue terry cloth bathing suits they made us swim in. Everyone also had to wear a tight-fitting cap before diving into the smelly indoor pool. We changed in the little cubicle dressing rooms and showered, feeling embarrassed, in the common shower stalls. After swimming we had pizza at a stand-up counter on the corner, while the traffic of people sped by us with the whir of revolving doors. With greasy pizza still on our fingers, we walked slowly through Azuma, sometimes trying on rings or long flowing scarves. Our day was over in time to watch the new soap opera, "One Life to Live," then "I Love Lucy." Every day we rushed home and sat cross-legged in front of the large TV in our room.

Living in New York again for the first time since I

was five both excited me and made me miss my friends. I went home for Marisol's birthday party and felt out of place. I remember sitting on the train alone, looking out the window and feeling that I was growing up: I was taking the train by myself. As I approached Westport I had the sensation of coming home and of not belonging at the same time. I thought that my three weeks away would have given all my friends the opportunity to forget about me. Other people were living in my house, so I couldn't sit on my bed and stare out the window, rub Smokey's stomach, or play the piano after everyone was asleep. I returned to Westport as a visitor.

It was a slumber party, and we stayed up all night, giggling and telling ghost stories, terrifying ourselves by conjuring up the spirits of famous dead people. We danced in the middle of the street as the sun rose. We fantasized what junior high would be like.

In August Gloria drove me to the airport and I boarded a small plane for Vermont. I was going to sleep-away camp for the first time. My suitcase was filled with a supply of Modess sanitary napkins which my mother had shown me how to use, just in case. The plane ride was bumpy and I was frightened. I was on my own. I ate the sandwich Gloria had made for me and felt sick to my stomach.


When my father brought us home from the summer, he came upstairs into our house for the first time since he had left. He touched everything lightly, as though checking for dust. I think he wanted to see if he was remembered there, even by the furniture. My mother had made some changes, moved beds around, and had the ugly bird wallpaper in the dining room painted over: one wall red, one white. My room surprised him the most, because it was filled with a twelve-year-old's life. It no longer had the bare sterility of a silent guest room or the cologne scent of the room he had occupied to distance himself from my mother. She wasn't home that day, and I felt as if we were two kids smoking cigarettes for the first time. I showed him what had once been *their* room, which was now very much *her* room, and its casual messiness produced in him a small, knowing laugh. We sat on my bed and he gave me an early birthday present: light blue personalized stationery which could be sealed with an embossed gold J. The sheets were lined with green fringe, and my name and address were printed in green.

"Now you have no excuse not to write me," he said.

"Well, you better write back!"

"I will," he said, rubbing my back.

"Thank you, Daddy," and I hugged him, hard.


His first letter from me was perhaps not the one he had been expecting. After only a few days in my new junior high I decided that the weekend upheaval was too jarring. I was in an "I love Westport" phase, and I thought New York was a disgusting place to live. I announced that no matter what my mother decreed, I would never leave Westport or my friends.

September 5, 1968

Dear Dad,

I really don't know how to say this. I am so afraid of hurting you. But . . . I have to tell you.

You see . . . well, I really don't want to go in every other weekend to New York. I just feel uncomfortable and wishing-I-was-home whenever I come.

You know how I feel about New York; that doesn't help me any. My place is at home. The place I love and cherish. This may be our last year in this house; I want it to last. And to just . . . well . . . I can't explain it. If we could make arrangements or something just so we are all happy, content, and satisfied. Please don't be angry. You are my Father; I love you. But you just have to understand me. . . .

Love, Julie

My father reacted better than I had anticipated. He told me that he understood, as long as we kept in touch and saw each other often enough. He said that if we had a feeling for each other we didn't need to prove it every other weekend.

September 18, 1968

Dear Daddy,

I think you are just simply magnifical. You are so understanding about the whole matter! I knew you would be.

I am so glad that you understand me. I think you are the only person that <u>really</u> does.

As for a correspondence, I'm entirely in favor of it. Now for some news!! School is so much fun this year! My favorite subjects are English and Spanish. . . .Well, don't forget to write and I love you.

Love, J.A.L.

P.S. If Ab comes in to NY could you have her bring me my allowance? It is $4.00 (I figured it out). Ab's is $1.20. If she doesn't, could you mail it to us please. I am broke. Thank you.

September 24, 1968

Dear Julie,

I received your letter on Monday morning—and can't tell you how pleased and happy you made me feel because

(1) you really believed that I understood what was happening to you—inside of you and outside of you—and that you will be able to trust my understanding more and more as time goes on—and

(2) that you can see—that two people who really love each other can manage to keep a good relationship going <u>even though</u> circumstances are such that they may not see a lot of each other for the time being.

It was wonderful to see you—and know that you are growing up with each new experience

(school, friends, boys, parties, etc.) and to ob-
serve how much you want to learn. The most
important thing in life is to <u>want</u> to experience
new situations and <u>to be able</u> to <u>learn</u> from
them. . . .

Keep well my beautiful big daughter—I think
of you all the time and love you with all my heart.

Daddy

One day I was looking through my mother's
jewelry box. My grandfather had given her a few
expensive pieces, and she had collected some out-of-
the-ordinary pins and heavy bracelets. She only wore
clip-on earrings because every time she got her ears
pierced they either got infected or she lost the earrings.
This day I came upon a ring I had never seen before.
It was a thick silver band beaten all the way around,
reminding me of a West Indian steel drum. Inside it
read "4-11 Till Death."

I showed the ring to my mother and asked her what
it was. A painful expression crossed her face briefly.
She told me it had been a present from her to my
father, one for each of them. April 11 was not their
anniversary, but rather the day that they had met.

"Till *death*?" I asked, incredulous.

"I was a real romantic, what can I say? So was your
father."

"Can I keep it for a while?"

"Okay, Julie. Do what you want with it."

I put it on my middle finger and wore it for months.

After finding this ring, I searched through the cabinets in the living room for my parents' wedding albums. There were two: one thick and white, the professionally put-together one; the other a wooden one with my parents' names spelled out in red leather letters. I turned the heavy pages slowly, wide-eyed at the young faces of my mother and father, my uncles and grandparents. Smokey came over and put her face on my lap, as if to comfort me.

I looked around our living room, which had been moved around since my father left. Since my mother had been spending time with Michael, he had helped her to rearrange the furniture and rid the house of the former interior decorator's work. Michael's bright influence could be felt everywhere. On the piano were vases of large dried Mexican flowers, and the rugs had been pulled back to reveal beautiful wood floors. I walked into the den, which had served as my father's office for a time. It was my favorite room in the house, the oldest, they told my parents when we bought it. There was even an oven for baking bread next to the fireplace. On one wall my mother hung pictures of us, of herself at work on stories for the paper. The room was still. It was a moment of assessment, and of longing for something I could not even name or remember. The sadness came; it stayed with me for a while and then I reluctantly let it go. Smokey and I left the den. I turned out the light.

# 13

Over the next two years, when I was twelve and thirteen, I was in junior high and there were new distractions and diversions. It was the circus of the late 60s and I was just old enough to be on the fringes.

I had my first kiss at a Valentine's Day dance, and I wore stockings and a bit of makeup. I shuffled my friends around weekly. I was becoming a teenager, and I think my mother was a little frightened of the responsibility. She never stopped reminding me that she had to be both mother and father to me now. Working at the newspaper full-time, my mother wasn't home at all during the day.

To ease the burden of running the house (and to assuage her own guilt for leaving us alone after school) my mother hired a young black woman from North Carolina to take care of us. Her name was

Victoria and she could neither read nor write. Victoria was 4'11" and weighed 250 pounds. We soon found out that Victoria was dyslexic, but full of common sense. She loved Abby and me, and we had a lot of fun together. Our family had also accumulated two cats, Charlie and Chastity (whom we called Kitty), a hamster named Cedric, and a series of parakeets who died at the rate of one per year.

My mother had never been the ordinary, run-of-the-mill type. Whereas most mothers brought their children toys or gave them clothes, nothing made my mother happier than presenting me with a large hard-back book or four thick paperbacks. If I was sick in bed or just because she felt like it, my mother would go to The Remarkable Bookshop, charge a bunch of books, and have them wrapped in brightly colored paper. I grew to love all the books she gave me: the smooth white pages, the new smell, the way they looked filling up my bookshelves. Abby didn't have the same immediate love for the books my mother brought her—she would much rather have had a set of felt-tip pens or a package of Reese's Peanut Butter Cups. Handing us our books, my mother would say, "They're for your lib'ry," and Abby and I would giggle at the way she always left out the second syllable of the word.

Sometimes my mother would stop at Bill's Smoke Shop on her way home from work and buy us each a pack of M & M's. She told us to save them for dessert, but when she was reading the paper in the den we would sneak up to Abby's room and shut the door behind us. We sat on the floor and opened the two packs of M & M's in front of us. Then we separated the little candies into color groups. There were red, green, orange, yellow, light brown, and dark brown: we both loved the reds and hated the dark brown.

My mother was not domestic and did not have the time to develop a talent for sewing, cooking, or gardening. She wrote theater reviews for the town newspaper and conducted interviews for long feature articles. Abigail and I often went with her to the Long Wharf and Yale Repertory theaters in New Haven to see plays. I never fell asleep without hearing the sound of her manual typewriter. It was a writer's lullaby. She had encouraged Abigail and me to write from the first time we were able to hold a pen (although she wasn't too pleased when I had taken my first red crayon and created a masterpiece on the walls of our New York apartment). I had been writing short stories since second grade, and in fourth grade I had won the school writing contest for my class. Whenever my friends came over, my mother would give us ideas for stories, and then she would read them and determine our prizes. Everyone always got the same prize, but the comments scrawled in the margin differed.

My mother rarely had time to cook dinner, so she either left me instructions on how to season the lamb chops or let Victoria make us a chuck steak. We insisted that my mother make the salad dressing every night because she used just the right amount of vinegar and garlic: we loved our mouths to burn as we ate it. Over the years my mother expanded her cooking repertoire. She had three meals which Abigail and I were supposed to be impressed with: chicken cacciatore, beef stew, and tarragon chicken and wine. On her chicken cacciatore nights, my mother believed in creating an entire mood. She would play an Italian opera at full volume and light the dining room with flickering candles. On these occasions we used colored cloth napkins instead of our regular paper ones, and if she really felt magnanimous, she would set the table with the Good Silver. My mother was a firm believer in "atmosphere," even for little girls.

Always accompanying the chicken were Mueller's Egg Noodles, a big green salad with cheese and apple slices, and rolls. My mother never completed a dinner without burning the rolls. She would put them in our huge black restaurant stove and promptly forget about them, so that right when we were salivating over our chicken the aroma of burned Pillsbury Doughboys would waft into the dining room. She would rush back into the kitchen, coughing from the smoke, and snatch the black remains out of the oven. The fan would spin furiously and if it was winter we would freeze for the rest of the meal. This process was repeated each time my mother prepared a meal with rolls. The noodles were always either overcooked or undercooked, and the butter was too hard to put on them anyway. The main dish was delicious, although I tend to think that this was pure luck.

My mother always left the job of cleaning up the masterpiece to Abby and me. She felt she had done her bit; it was back up to her typewriter after that. As we cleaned, onion skins slid out of corners and pieces of garlic stuck tenaciously in the holes of the garlic press. We could never find tops for the wine bottles, and empty tomato paste cans rolled back and forth on the floor. We would spend a lot of time unsticking carrot peels from the wall next to the garbage pail— her aim wasn't too good either. In spite of all this, we were proud of our mother when she made the effort.

My mother passed very little of her culinary knowledge on to me. I was supposed to absorb as much culture as possible. I was to be well-read, able to identify any composer while listening to WQXR, and know the difference between Renaissance and Impressionist painters. But when it came to sewing a hem or making beef bourguignon, there was a large gap in my education.

At least once a week I heard my mother say that she wanted nothing more than for Abigail and me to have a good relationship with our father. She blamed him for never taking the time to be with us alone anymore. She didn't understand why he had to bring his entire entourage along every time we saw him. Even my letters to him were always signed "send my love to Gloria and Company" or "give my regards to Broadway (and Gloria, Kelly, Amy, David, Steven, and Samantha)." He had become a part of a family which only sometimes included Abigail and me. In those days whenever my mother criticized my father, I defended him. It was often an involuntary response: I just felt the need to contradict anything she said about him, even if I believed she was right. I thought she was too quick to judge him. However, without

being aware of it, I was slowly beginning to incorporate my mother's values into my own. As time
went on, I had a difficult time taking my father's side
about anything.

The relationship that was developing between my
sister and me was perhaps different from that between
most sisters. If there were any givens in my life,
the first was that I loved her more than anyone else
in the world.

Because my mother was not at home as much as
Abigail and I were, I watched out for my sister in
many cases as though I were her mother. I was very
protective of her; I wanted to shield her from pain. It
wasn't that my mother didn't do her job of mothering
and loving Abigail to the fullest, for she always did.
My role was a self-imposed one; *I* interpreted what
my duties and responsibilities were.

Abigail was lazy when it came to eating. If nothing
was put in front of her, she would not make an effort
to find anything. She simply would not eat. While
she was watching "Let's Make a Deal" on TV, I
would make her a tuna fish sandwich and prepare a
tray with a Coke, a napkin, Fritos, and a couple of
Oreos on the side and bring it up to her room. I liked
waiting on her and enjoyed taking care of her.

I helped her with her homework and we played
games together, interviewing each other on my
mother's new tape recorder. I was always the straight
man, the interviewer, and she created several roles for

herself: Hilda Herrington, the famous book critic; Sam, the toilet cleaner; a European actress; a window washer. Abigail had many voices and a knack for impersonation.

Her best friend's name was Ellise. When they were in the first grade I told them we were going to play a game called the Beverly Hillbillies. The rules of this game called for Abby and Ellise to stay in their nightgowns after they had woken up. Then I would blindfold them, spin them around, and put them outside just when the mailman was delivering the mail. Taking off their blindfolds, they would scream and giggle and tear up the stairs to Abby's room. They loved this game, and even after they were too old to want to play it anymore, they always reminded me of the good old Beverly Hillbilly days when they were young.

Abigail and I had a tendency to make fun of our mother, to mimic her when she wasn't looking and imitate the way she looked at herself in the mirror. Whereas I was considered sullen and serious, Abigail was funny, witty. The older she got, the more pointed her humor became. She could make me laugh when no one else could, and she did the same for her friends. Everyone loved her, for she was a maverick: the kind of person who would put on my mother's old push-up bra and stockings, long black gloves, and the high heels my mother had saved for fifteen years waiting for them to come back in style, and parade around the living room; who would talk earnestly to her reflection in the mirror, lamenting the imperfections that had the nerve to find their way to *her* face. She was the kind of kid who did her homework lying on the stairs, her math book propped up on the landing. She would talk on the phone for hours, pacing back and forth in the kitchen, wrapping the wire around her waist, picking at the salad while I made it. She never sat at a desk, rarely cried, and took up tap dancing rather than ballet. She declared that she would "tip-tap her way to Broadway." She understood me, she knew my moods. We stuck together.

However, in dealing with my father, it was I who represented the feelings of both of us to him. At this time, Abigail never spoke about her true feelings or her attitude toward him. I would be the one to call and say that we weren't coming in that weekend. I was the one who was brought to tears after every conversation. Perhaps I did not give her the chance. I did everything because I was older.

I still believe that Abby has always felt things more deeply than she reveals. Beginning when she was about nine, she began screaming in her sleep in the middle of the night. I would be asleep in my room and through the closed door I could hear a frantic "No! No! No!" a muffled, terrified sound. I would run into her room to find her head buried under the covers, her hands clenched. Gently awakening her, I would say, "It's all right, Ab, it's all right." She would open her eyes with a disoriented expression on her face and moan a bit. I would hug her and rub her back until she fell asleep. Usually she didn't remember any of this in the morning, but sometimes she could recall fragments of dreams: someone trying to suffocate her, black spiders crawling over her, a person she couldn't recognize chasing her. My mother rarely came in because she couldn't hear the screams; her room was beyond mine and ever since her labyrinthitis she had lost sixty percent of her hearing in one ear. Abby told me she was afraid and asked me if I would leave my door open at night. I did and heard her cries each time they occurred. Sometimes she sleepwalked into my room, asking me for scissors or cameras. Guiding her back to her room, I would tuck her in firmly and she would fall right asleep.

# 14

July 2, 1969

Dear Daddy,

I got your letter today. I thank you for sending me and Ab the six-page "little note."

Daddy, I'm so glad that you are happy when I'm happy because sometimes I feel guilty having a lot of fun on the weekends I should be with you. But I know that in your whole body there is not one selfish bone so I feel all right. And also, I never said your APARTMENT (as you call it) in N.Y. was crowded. Your house is beautiful and I love it. I'm sure everyone that lives there loves it too.

I knew you wouldn't be mad, hurt, insulted, etc., if I didn't come to New York but I thought you might feel I liked Westport and my friends, or rather _loved_ Westport and my friends more than you, but oh Daddy I love you so much, but

I don't know, we haven't been getting along too well lately and I feel so guilty. I know I am changing in a million and one ways but I don't think you know. If I wear eyeliner or something I think I should be able to without you teasing me about it. I know you're only joking but you make me feel so self-conscious. Also if I don't see you in about a month or so and then I see you—you always seem to remark about how I'm changing or that I'm taller, fatter, uglier, beautifuler, or something. I know that you mean well, but please —I live with myself and I know. . . .

I don't think that there is any other person in the whole world who would say what you said about the "newsy" calls (how they aren't satisfying). You are so right! You are the most understanding person I know. You feel out everybody else's thoughts—that's one reason why you are the great man that you are.

And, Daddy, if I act stand-offish or like a snob in front of you it's because, well, I'm sort of self-conscious in front of you. Believe me that's not my real self. I think our relationship is a very good, close one, but I don't see you for a long time sometimes (because of my own decision) and then when I do see you—we are like distant relatives.

Oh, Daddy, I have such deep thoughts about your's and Mom's divorce I could not even begin to tell you. But it comes out in the way I act when I see you. But please remember I'll always love you—even if you did something terrible—

because you are my father—part of you is in me and I'll never forget that!
I'll always love you—
Julie

P.S. I'm sorry I cried at your wedding when you were so happy. I was selfish. . . .

Two months later, I became thirteen, and the year ahead was an unlucky one for me. The difficulties I was having with my father were small in comparison to the new, strained relationship between my mother and me. As I wrote my father repeatedly, I was changing; the problem was that my mother did not like the person I was becoming. I surrounded myself with friends and what she considered "frivolous" activities. My life at school was everything to me, and I pulled away from her and the outings she liked the three of us to go on as a "family." I covered my walls with "Eugene McCarthy For President" stickers and peace signs. I began to take an interest in boys and even "went steady": I wore his heavy silver ID on my wrist with his name engraved on the outside, mine on the inside. Each romance lasted a month or two at most, but the notes we passed in math and Spanish classes were fevered.

I did not confide in my mother or sister during this period and it seemed to her that I considered myself superior to her rule. In a sense I did, because my life at school occupied me more than my mother's pleas for me to accompany her to my grandparents' house. My mother could not bear being shut out. She thought it reflected her inadequacies as a mother. She disapproved of me and my "egocentric" ways. She made me volunteer at an after-school child-care center in Norwalk, and she drove me there herself, once a week, determined that I help somebody other than myself. We had a foster child in the Philippines from the Save the Children Federation, and Abby and I were supposed to help support her and write monthly.

The more my mother disciplined me and expressed her frustration with my misguided character, the farther I pulled away from her. It was not a hostile act, although in her desire to be an understanding, compassionate, and needed mother, she interpreted my behavior in that way. Because she was a writer, and because our verbal confrontations resulted in screams and tears, we began an inter-room correspondence. After a particularly loud or brittle interchange I would hear a slight slip under my closed door and a two-page, single-spaced letter from my mother would have appeared. She always typed them on her manual typewriter on light brown, first-draft paper—all in one exasperated exhalation, it seemed to me.

Julie, please don't tell me not to come in your room—again, I repeat, this is my home, and you don't call the shots, you don't make the rules, and I mean it. Our relationship cannot start fresh now, because I don't accept your terms and never will. I respect your desire to be yourself, but you show me who you are first, not just a spoiled little girl who just wants to talk on the phone, buy clothes, and be with boys—because if that's what you want to be, then I say that's a kind of person for whom I have no respect.

As far as your point about going places with me and Abigail . . . you are part of a family—in five years you will be away from us in college and will still be fortified by your family and its values. You are not living in a vacuum; you are part of a whole, and a very decent entity it is . . . someday, hopefully, you will realize this.

A couple of months later a letter like this was slid under my door:

That's what the business of being parent and child is all about: giving and taking, loving. Think about how I am reacting to you when you are cruel—your refusal to join in family things . . . if you know it gives comfort to go together as a family occasionally . . . so why not do so to give happiness . . . must you always take and suck someone else's giving dry? I will always be your friend when others change and withdraw. I am not an enemy, but you seem to make the contest one of wills. I am not out to break yours, but to mold a character, to help you find the person you are. So no more insolence. If I do ask you to accompany the family somewhere, think before you automatically answer violently in the negative . . . put yourself in my place, a mother who loves her girls, who finds one turning her face at her kiss, uninterested in spending time with her or her family. . . .

At first my mother sensed me drifting from what she insisted on calling "the family." Her adamancy only succeeded in alienating me further, because although I loved them both, I did not want to be around my mother a lot. I was going through the first in a series of "identity crises." My mother was perceptive enough to realize this, so she tried to influence me with her values. The family was value number one: perhaps overly defensive because our family was different from others, my mother could not bear my thirteen-year-old rejection of all that she could offer me. Maybe she felt guilty about the strange structure of our lives and did not want me to come out of it a casualty. She wanted me to be well-adjusted.

Aside from my confusion about my friends, my journal from this year does not record a great unhappiness. I continued going in to see my father. Grandma Sallie had become ill with cancer by this point. Her long hair was cut and she looked frail, thin.

March 29, 1970
Saturday we went to New York. I saw everyone. Dad let Kelly and me smoke in the restaurant! Today Grandma Sallie came over. God she looks like shit. I feel like a part of me is gone.

In spite of my mother's judgmental attitude toward me, I did not feel wholly antagonistic toward her.

March 31, 1970
I think that Mom and Michael ought to get mar-

ried. I respect Michael and wouldn't mind having him for a stepfather. Dad is really great—I really love him all the way. Steven and David, too.

The issue quickly turned into one of trust. It was the height of the drug era and Westport's Needle Park was notorious as the spot for many exchanges. My mother was sure that I was going to turn to drugs. She believed that I was so impressionable and lost that I would consider marijuana a solution to my problems. As a warning, she wrote:

> I would really feel that I had failed in many ways if I found that you felt you needed the stuff . . . that you were too bored or not excited enough about the promise of life and all the things you could give and get from it that you would want to indulge in something that has been proven an utter retreat and escape . . . and of course a deadly entrance to an inevitable death of one sort or another . . . of the soul or the body.

The more my mother disciplined me, the angrier she became that my father wasn't helping her. She didn't confide in him; they rarely spoke, and when they did their voices were sharp and caustic. There was not one telephone conversation where my father did not hang up on my mother, unable to face her accusations. "You never call the girls, you never *do* anything special with them, you aren't being a good father," she would tell him. "Stop telling me what to

do, stop judging me, stop acting so superior!" he
would yell before slamming down the phone. My
mother disapproved of my father more than of me.
He was old enough to know better, whereas I was just
someone who hadn't gotten her morals straight.

I try to be so many things [she wrote]. A good
mother, an accomplished professional, a good
warm potential wife to Michael (and he is indeed
as though a husband to me). A good man, as they
say, is hard to find. . . . So many men are cruel
to their wives' offspring from other marriages . . .
I have been careful . . . and consider myself more
than lucky to love a man who loves me, who loves
my children, even though sometimes they are not
so lovable. . . .
    The world is crumbling from people who
think only about themselves . . . and if you don't
learn now . . . some kind of commitment to your
family you will never learn. . . . So, I repeat, some
kind of emotional commitment to your family is
the beginning of how you relate later in life.

My mother expected too much from me. It was as
though I were a guitar and she tightened the strings
more and more, afraid of losing me entirely. She was
intent upon strengthening the walls of our triangle
and she treated me as though I were a much older person, capable of understanding her complex emotions
as well as my own. I wondered where my childhood

had gone. Why couldn't I just play in the park in my underwear, why didn't Daddy roll down the hill in the backyard with me, why was everything so complicated?

The first time I tried marijuana in the eighth grade my mother found out immediately. Three pages of light brown typing paper were slid under my door, and as I read them I cried so hard I refused to come out for hours, unable to face her.

What did you really do Sunday afternoon? If you consider yourself a rebel, forget it—rebellion takes strength and courage. You are simply, it seems, pulled and pushed by every force you encounter . . . full of intelligence and sensitivity, you seem unable to apply it to developing a code of life of your own. Are you going to plead a rotten life or the broken-home bit? If so, examine it carefully. Both your father and I love you and consider your welfare and mental and physical comforts constantly. Your sister loves and respects you, and Michael as well, and Grandma and Grandpa. I am most utterly disappointed in you. . . . You and I as mother and daughter have nothing going or very little at most, if you cannot discuss this experimentation with me. If you can't talk to me about this, then discuss it with your father. For certainly after we talk about this I will relate this to him. I feel too deeply about you to let you fall into these self-destructive habits— and I do . . . very deeply.

May 17, 1970
My mother found out about me smoking. How I
don't know. On Thursday night she gave me one
of her famous letters and left. I went into hys-
terics. . . . I called Steven who really helped me.
I was scared and crying, no, sobbing. Shit it was
awful. She was going to ground me for two
weeks, but she called Dad and they decided on
just this weekend, I guess. So I missed out on two
fantastic parties but I think I'll survive.

After receiving this letter, I had the terrible sensation of having let my mother down, of "deceiving"
her in a way that would never let her forgive me. I
didn't think that what I had done was so horrible, but
she made me feel that I was a weak and inconsequential person. I couldn't talk to my father about all of
this. I didn't know whose side he would be on and I
didn't want to risk it. For once I thought that it would
be the two of them against me, although I doubted
that. I was left with a despair, believing I was not a
*good* person.

The rest of that school year I experimented with
different personalities as one would try on frilly costumes in a dressing room. Nothing seemed to fit: I
gave up the "frivolous" one my mother had con-
demned and stopped wearing makeup and nice
clothes. I turned to a different group of friends who
were considered "hippies" or "freaks" in junior high
school. They discussed drugs and Bob Dylan, Bud-
dhism and Jack Kerouac. Among them, people did

not "go steady" or even go out one on one. Everything was done in groups and we all wore BVD T-shirts and blue jeans. I put the mattress from my bed on the floor and pasted photographs from *Life* magazine on the walls. I found little solace there, for I didn't belong naturally; I merely assumed a role among them. This person didn't please my mother either, for she was convinced that this path led to irresponsibility and apathy.

However, by the end of the school year I had forgiven her and was willing to accept that perhaps her values were not so terrible.

June 25, 1970
My mother is talking about me. I love her . . .
Jacqui claims she has the best relationship with her mother over anyone. Although Mom's and mine is very good . . .

No matter how insistent my endeavors to grow up, I found that I was held back by one fundamental pain that I could do nothing about. My troubles finding a "group" to belong to in school were secondary to the issue that hurt me more than any other.

Spring, 1970
Dear Daddy,
Hi. When I read your letter, at first I just sat there. Then I read it again and started crying. This week was crying week. . . .
Listen, you know I need you here whether I'm growing up or not. How do you think I feel, see-

ing people with their fathers, talking with their fathers, saying: "My father did this, etc." Don't you think I wish you lived with us? When Mom and I are in a fight, who do you think I turn to? No one. My friends don't understand; they are great people but not for guiding me. I only have myself and I can't console myself all of the time. I never (here I go crying again) will know what it's like for you to come home, sit down, read the paper, eat dinner. I always wish for a routine kind of thing but it's never there. I am grateful for everything I have, don't get me wrong. But I have problems with friends, school, boys, and I just don't tell Mom. I would tell you if you were here—I know I would. . . .

The way Kelly is growing up and the way I'm growing up are a lot different. I wish you could be with me while I grow up too, but if you and Mom "dislike each other immensely" there's nothing anyone can do. . . .

And, Dad, I have changed a lot and I still like Westport but I like NY too. I want to spend some time in New York and especially with you, Gloria, and company. . . .

Well, write back if you want . . . I really miss Steven and David. We are so close but I never see them and it seems they relate better with Kelly now. They mean a lot to me and I need them, as I need you. I do talk a lot, don't I?

Well, bye now.

Love always, Julie

I knew then that the problems I was having determining my "social identity" in school were not a direct result of the confusion and unhappiness I felt about not growing up with my father. Every thirteen- or fourteen-year-old has a difficult time releasing childhood and gracefully assuming the role of an adult. There was little grace in this period for me. There was a slight hint of rebellion against the kind of person I thought my mother wanted me to be, but I was really only reaching out for a very normal and routine foundation to fall back on. All that I desired were a stable family, clear-cut love, and uncomplicated relationships. Even though the preservation of our abbreviated family was my mother's primary objective, she could not give me back simplicity. My mother and father could not undo what had been done, love each other again, and live in the same house. With each year the lives of my two parents pulled farther apart and the memories of our family life grew dimmer. Sometimes my unhappiness stemmed not only from dealing with a current situation, but from wondering about what *could* have been, imagining the kind of life I *might* have had. I did not blame my parents for my novel life, for I knew that their divorce was preferable to the fighting and open hatred that had passed between them before. I never thought that they should have remained married for our sake. It was the aftermath of the divorce which created the real problems for me.

# 15

It was 1970. My father was supposed to spend the month of August with Abigail and me. This year he decided to combine his three families in a house he had bought in Amagansett, Long Island. It was a gray-shingled house at the bottom of a long hill, very clean and modern inside. Kelly and I were almost fourteen, and we were to share a large room with twin beds and red, white, and blue bedspreads. Amy and Abigail had a smaller room, and Steven an even smaller one on the side. A long upstairs living room separated the bedrooms, and on the walls my father had hung his favorite pictures of his children. Sometimes while Kelly and Steven were making macramé bracelets I would lie on the couch, looking up at the pictures. I had scrutinized these same pictures all my life, and I never tired of them.

For the first time, all six kids attempted to live together under the same roof for more than a weekend. David was nineteen then and he was there with his Australian girl friend, so he didn't spend as much time with us as he might have. In the beginning, the situation seemed ideal: we could walk to the beach, fend for ourselves during the day, and do anything we wanted to at night. The beach was full of kids our age and older. Kelly and Steven joined a group of them immediately. I didn't feel quite right with them. I never thought that I fit in. As a result, at the beach I was usually very quiet in large groups, and I stayed up in my room reading often. I loved walking on the sand in the early morning before the people came, picking over dead crabs for sea glass and shells. My father collected blue and green glass which had been softened and worn smooth by the waves. It was a summer of marijuana smoking, and after the encounter with my mother, I was not so anxious to join in. But one night a small group of us slept out in the dunes, smoking dope, cooking hot dogs, and roasting marshmallows in a fire. I began to feel more at ease.

I thought that Abigail was unhappy there: she was ten, not quite old enough to be with the "big kids," and the little kids were too young for her. Emotionally it was a highly charged time, an experiment of sorts. I remember thinking that here was the time I was supposed to be spending with my father, *living* together once more, and instead I was thrust into a large group of kids. Gloria's participation that month was shadowy; she was a neutral force in the beginning. She didn't try to discipline Abigail or me, whereas she was quite strict with her own daughters. I don't believe that we were ever a working family. Everyone had lives other than the ones here, and somehow the combination of all of us did not jell. On the surface, Gloria and my father seemed in control of the mixture of children. I did not sense any struggle going on between them behind closed doors, although later I learned differently.

When the time came for Abigail and me to leave to go back to Westport, we wanted to stay a bit longer. I was finally beginning to enjoy myself. We had only been there for three weeks and I asked for a few more days. For some reason I could not comprehend, the answer was no. Feeble excuses were made, and I was accused of being sour and not helpful enough, but my father gave me no concrete explanation. He and I had a long and heated argument as I stood before him with tears streaming down my face. I wondered why this man always had the power to make me cry. One look, one word, and all the pain I thought I had buried rose to the surface in a moment. When I cried, I became flustered and felt I could not hold my ground.

I found out later that he had wanted us to stay, but Gloria had not. She had been complaining to him about us for the entire three weeks, and when they discussed the question of our staying a bit longer, she insisted that she wanted that time for the four of them to be alone. Finally, they decided we could stay, but by then it was too late. Once my father's pride had been wounded, his will was resolute, scathing. That he should have to fight for the right of his own children to stay in *his* house angered him perhaps more than anything he had known previously with Gloria. He considered her hesitations to be a direct insult against his children. My father drove Abigail and me to the ferry. He sat alone in the front seat and the two of us cried in the back for the whole trip. No one said a word.

The explosion at the end of the summer was, in essence, the end for Gloria. Although I did not know it at the time, their marriage had not been as wonderful as it had appeared, and the attempt to merge our families had been too much. These were things I was not consciously aware of when I was thirteen; I simply felt that everything was not quite right. My father's silences, his heaviness, were hints of a hidden sadness which he did not reveal to me until he and Gloria decided to get a divorce.

I entered the ninth grade with a different kind of resolve. My "frivolous" self having been discarded, the "hippie" costume ill-fitting, I withdrew from everyone into myself.

I hid behind my long hair and the silver-rimmed hexagonal glasses I wore at the time. I spent most afternoons in my room, reading novels by D. H. Lawrence and Philip Roth. Some days, when it was warm enough, I collected wildflowers from the backyard, identifying them from a book Abigail had given me for my birthday. I went back to playing the piano and

took up the recorder. I wrote poetry. I hooked rugs
and knit scarves. Aside from my few friends, and my
mother, sister, and Victoria, it was a solitary life. It is
only now, looking back and attempting to reconstruct
the events which had their effect on me, that I see why
I became so sad and withdrawn. At the time I imagined
that there was something wrong with me, that I was
a misfit.

In October of that year, my father met another
woman. Somehow Gloria found out about it, and in
late January he moved out. They began their divorce
proceedings in the spring. I was confused; Abigail and
I stopped going in to visit them. There were long
silences. The only letters I sent my father were to pass
on to him pictures of himself in the army which I had
found among my mother's papers. He moved to the
Hotel Esplanade on the West Side. We heard stories
of how terrible Gloria was being, how after three
years of marriage and no children between them, she
was trying to "get him for all he was worth." She de-
manded an exorbitant alimony, he said, and she had
sold the house in Amagansett. She wanted to keep
their most valuable paintings, the ones my father had
bought to start his impressive collection. My father
loved those paintings, and Gloria's insistence on keeping them infuriated him. Once again I saw love
reduced to dividing up possessions, arguing about
financial compensation. This time there were no visiting rights to determine, for my father intended to
renounce Gloria's entire family. Unfortunately, we
were supposed to also. Just as my father attempted to

erase Gloria from his life, we were to end our relationship with her and her two daughters. One day we had a stepmother and two stepsisters. The next day we didn't. I was angry at Gloria for making so many demands on my father, but she had never done anything against me *directly*. I certainly had no resentment against Kelly and Amy. They, like us, were merely victims of their parents' whims and incompatibilities. Abigail's and my weekend life temporarily ceased, and we tried to make sense out of our father's decisions.

I never felt comfortable about the fact that we stopped seeing Gloria and her children so abruptly. I was too young to stand up for my own feelings and too swayed by my father's demands for loyalty to him. This "loyalty" issue disturbed me, for it implied that blood love was more powerful and enduring than any other kind. For three years the message had been subtly conveyed to me that I should make an effort to love this woman, my father's new wife, and her two daughters. And now there was a prohibition on love for them, an edict, in effect, banishing them from our family. My anger is stronger now than it was then. At the time I followed my father's wishes and did not call or write to them. In March, Abigail and I received this letter:

Dear Julie and Abigail,
I thought of calling you last week but I felt I couldn't handle the call emotionally.
I just want to say to both of you that I truly miss you, dear Julie, and you, sweet Abigail, and

if at any time you would like to visit us, please
feel free to call.

Fondly,<br>
Gloria

My father scoffed at this letter. He was very bitter,
suspicious. So we didn't tell him that for every birthday for years after this, Gloria sent Abigail and me
sweet cards.

To this day I do not know how Gloria really felt
about us, the additional four children she acquired
when she married my father. All I know is what my
father has told me. Their battles in court have not
ended, even now. I have not seen Gloria since 1971.

# 16

My only goal at this point was to finish junior high school and go on to high school. My mother and I had been getting along better because I was pursuing the "higher interests" she valued. She thought I was to be admired for the ability to spend a lot of time alone. "Some people get to be forty and have never been alone," she told me. "You should be proud of yourself."

Michael was spending more time at our house, sometimes sleeping over in the downstairs bedroom. But still our primary family consisted of my mother, Abigail, and me. I stopped fighting them so much. We were going to Europe at the end of June; my mother wanted to expose us to the beauties and antiquities of another way of life. She thought we were becoming too narrow, too provincial. For the first time, I was truly excited about something.

Just before school was out, Abigail and I met Carol. My father had called and said that since he didn't have anywhere for us to come to visit him, could he drive up and spend the day with us? We agreed. As an afterthought, he added, "I'm going to bring Carol because I'd like you to meet her, okay?"

From the minute I saw her pointy-toed white sneakers and ankle socks, I knew that I wasn't going to like her. She sat with her knees bent under her in straight-leg jeans in the front seat of my father's new brown Mercury Montego, her blond hair curled, her lips outlined in red. Other than that, she wore no makeup on her fair skin and her pale blue eyes blinked widely at us. She appeared to be in her early thirties, a "down home on the ranch" type of woman, although she told us she was an actress.

"Your Dad has told me so much about you two," she warbled. I hated it when people said "your Dad." She chattered the whole time, and Abigail and I looked at each other uncomfortably in the back seat. We had lunch at Chubby Lane's, a serve-yourself hamburger place in Westport. While Carol talked, I looked at the designs on the wallpaper. My father acted differently with Carol than he had with Gloria. He was quieter, calmer. She pampered him and he loved it.

We left for London not long after this meeting. Before leaving, we learned that my father had found an apartment on the Upper West Side. He and Carol were living there together.

The trip to Europe was wonderful. We visited friends in London, Paris, Liechtenstein, and Zurich.

I was absorbed by the history of London (I loved the idea of standing on the spot where Anne Boleyn's head was chopped off!), the excitement of Paris. In Liechtenstein we stayed with the president of the country and his family because his wife was an American woman who had studied French with my mother. We climbed mountains and immersed ourselves in the different life-styles, the big meals at noon, naps afterward, driving on narrow country roads. Except for a couple of fights with my mother, I was happy and enthusiastic about being in Europe. My journal is full of my observations, my awareness of the world which was so much larger than my family and me. There is not one mention of my father or Carol, and I only wrote him two postcards. One is addressed to him alone, but with "Give my regards to Carol" at the bottom; the second addressed to him with "& Carol" written in small letters below. They are stiff, informative notes.

The three weeks in Europe were a delightful respite from the intensity of the months before. It was a chance for me to forget my unhappiness at school and the unease I felt about my father and Gloria, my father and Carol. I returned home apprehensive, anxious now that the carefree weeks were over.

Michael was a gentle and sensitive man. He understood me in a way that my own father didn't. But he never attempted to replace my father; his relationship to Abigail and me was straightforward and loving.

When we first met him, he lived in a renovated barn in Westport, a gray house shadowed by tall trees. He filled his home with plants, colorful pots and pans, and a dove named Maud who flew from perch to perch. Michael had drawn my portrait in charcoal when I was seven. I remember sitting stiffly in a director's chair in his studio, holding on to the arms and not daring to breathe. Michael drew this before he and my mother started seeing each other, before the divorce. Later, he did two more charcoal drawings —one of me and one of Abigail. The only difference is that I have lost my two long braids and my eyes are not quite as shy.

Michael's participation in our lives was understated. He shared our worries, helped celebrate our successes. For Halloween one year two friends of mine and I were going to be the Jack, Queen, and King of Hearts. On two large pieces of cardboard he painted me the Jack of Hearts, and I paraded from door to door, proud of my signed sandwich boards. Another time I had to do an English project with photographs and a story line matted on poster paper. My mother and grandfather posed for me as characters in the story, and Michael took the starring role, as well as helping me to design and photograph the project. One Christmas he allied himself with Abigail and me and persuaded our mother to allow us to have a tree—a small one, he assured her, but he had been raised as a Catholic and Christmas had meant much to him; couldn't she bend her will of tradition just once? My mother finally gave in. On Christmas Eve, after

Abigail and I had fallen asleep counting Santas, they bought a skinny, short tree and decorated it in the middle of the den. My mother laid prestrung cranberries over the branches and stuck in a few cellophane-wrapped popcorn balls. I think she may even have enjoyed herself. Michael created his own ornaments: he hung paper cutouts symbolizing our presents on the ends of the fragile branches. When Abigail and I came down the next morning, we were thrilled. This was as real a Christmas as we were ever going to get. Michael was modest in the morning, his low voice lower. It was a happy Christmas; my mother glowed.

The summer between my seventh- and eighth-grade years, my mother, sister, grandparents, and I went to Provincetown for two weeks. Michael had joined us at the beginning of the second week, and he drove us from beach to beach in his jeep. He rode the waves with the rest of us, getting brown and healthy, losing the pallor he had acquired from long hours in his studio. He was one of us; I felt no resentment, no tension.

Michael never moved in with us completely, and I didn't know if that was his decision or my mother's. Actually I knew very little and was quite naive about my mother's and Michael's entire relationship. She told me his art came before anything else, that often the triangle of the three of us was too tight for him to be a part of in a complete sense. He encouraged her with her writing, and she finally sat down to write a book; he helped her to believe in *her* art. His artwork filled our walls, unusual, sophisticated paintings and collages which were ahead of their time. Michael accompanied us on all family functions, and he attempted to get along with and to understand my grandparents. They did not have the same prejudice against him as they had against my father. Because my grandfather was an art collector, Michael had won their good graces merely by being an artist.

When I entered high school, he was around our house less and less. I continued my solitary approach in this new school, taking acting class and Spanish, English, math, and chemistry. I started out with a coldness in me, and I didn't know where it came from. I made an effort to be enthusiastic in school, but I felt shy, confused. Throughout the fall I was not entirely unhappy; I was challenged by my schoolwork and excited to meet new people. There is not one mention of my father or Carol in my journal, and no letters passed between us. I don't remember going to see them very often. Relations were not necessarily strained, merely nonexistent.

Sometime in January I asked my mother where Michael had been, why we hadn't seen much of him, why there were only three at our dinner table again. She looked distressed. She was beginning to get that thin, pinched look she had had five years before. She told me that they had decided to stop seeing each other, that he was too dedicated to his work and couldn't *give* enough to her, that she had held on waiting for him in some way too long and it was over. He was gone. "But will we ever see him again?" I asked her, on the verge of tears.

"That will be up to you," she said. "There is still love between us, but it's just not working. He has helped me enormously but I've got to do it on my own now. He loves you and Abigail very much—don't forget that."

January 31, 1972
The last day of a cold-hot month. I had quite an emotional weekend, but I didn't write any of it in here, which, I suppose, is typical of me . . . I didn't have my period so I don't know why I was depressed and teary. . . . Last night I was thinking about it, and thinking of calling Dad (Was it last night? Night ideas seem ridiculous in the day) and when he would ask, "What has been going on?" I would, or could, have said (1) Mom's book (2) Michael's gone (3) looking at Mom and Dad's wedding pictures (unimportant but might hold significance) (4) Mom's depression and alienation from me. It was only when I broke down and cried that she actually talked to me and I loved her then. She comforted me marvelous much. It's true though that she is so wrapped up in her own problems and fears that she is ignoring us. I can understand her fear and moods, but I still crave attention.

For ten days of my sophomore year in February, 1972, I went to London with the drama group in school. Once again, when far away from home and the changes that were occurring in our family, I reveled in the freedom and beauty of Europe. The days were gray and rainy, but the nights were filled with great theater: we saw Laurence Olivier in *Long Day's Journey into Night*, Alec Guinness, Albert Finney, and Diana Rigg in other plays. It was a rich time, and when the ten days were over I was not anxious to return to school.

Once back in the routine, my mother, Abigail, and I were alone again. Victoria had returned to North Carolina and we had a new housekeeper from Jamaica who cried loudly at night, missing her family. My mother had switched jobs, and she was working on a newly formed newspaper with a more liberal point of view. Abigail was halfway through her sixth grade year at a free school, The Learning Community, and had already performed in *The Bald Soprano* and witnessed a hysterectomy on a dog.

There were long silences from my father. My mother fumed about that, and I often agreed with her. As time went on, I came to believe that whatever she said was almost completely right. At the dinner table we talked about the war in Vietnam, prison reform, the upcoming election. My mother was passionately interested in everything; she cried while watching the news on television. "You've got to help other people in this world," she would say. It all sank in slowly. I listened and watched and tried to piece together what *I* believed in. My father played no part in my political or moral education. My mother was coming into her own.

Not having a man around the house meant that my

mother had to take charge of everything. With each year in our enormous house, the upkeep and the worries increased. The gutters had to be cleaned, the lawn kept in shape (the garden had withered long before), the storm windows put up and taken down, the pipes kept from bursting. My mother paid the taxes, the heating bills, and the doctor bills. She bought our clothes and food and took care of all our extras. My father sent her alimony and child support every month; a thin envelope with a yellow check was supposed to arrive on the first—it usually appeared on the sixth. Abigail and I no longer received an allowance from my father; we were entirely dependent upon our mother.

My father was generous with us if we asked him for something. For our birthdays he bought us stereos and clock radios, typewriters and cameras. He paid for my contact lenses in April of that year. For the most part, however, my mother balanced our lives; she took care of our emotional and physical well-beings. It angered her that my father did not play a stronger role in our lives at this point. She was worried that we needed a male model; she was concerned how we would relate with men later on. Carol and my father were living happily in New York with three cats. It seemed to me that they were "playing house."

> March 13, 1972
> 54 Bond St. NYC

Very Dear Julie and Very Dear Ab,

It was important that you sort of got your bearings before I wrote to you but time has passed now and I just want you to know—(as a matter of fact) I think it's very important that you know that though our situation has changed, the love has not.

I think of you constantly—snow, a clap of thunder, Bette Davis on TV, Ruby Keeler and tap shoes, the TV Queen Elizabeth series, and Europe or . . . and whatever.

Please believe that problems of life-change have nothing to do with <u>removal of love</u>—it's more a matter of mathematics—like 3 and 1 sometimes cannot make 4 but also $1+1+1+1$ or $3+1$ or $2+2$ or $1+3$ have nothing to do with love.

I love you all $1+1+1+1$ or $3+1$ or $2+2$ or $1+3$.

Love to all three of you, xxx
Michael

He said it—the three of us plus the one of him could not make four. Were we that imposing? Drawn tightly together, we were a support system, a very female entity. I missed him. It was as though my mother had just been through her second divorce. She went out occasionally, but she was working constantly on her book and at the paper.

Abigail still didn't talk much about her feelings. Her nightmares continued, but she could never remember what they had been about. I must have appeared strange to my sister. I was not a "typical teenager." I didn't go out a lot, drink or smoke or spend all night on the phone. Without realizing it,

I believe I was adapting myself to my mother's solitude.

As summer approached we had to decide about renting the house, about what to do for the months ahead. Once again my mother wanted to rent it and I objected.

June 6, 1972

I was telling Jacqui and myself long before that I have an abnormal fixation for this house. I was trying to decide if it was because I was "happy" here in a real family situation, or just because it is so beautiful and us and ours. I don't want other people to live in it. I think it's an unhealthy and restricting feeling, but that's how I feel.

We did not rent the house that summer. I was relieved, but when I learned I was going to spend a month in Europe, it wasn't as important anyway. My mother's grandmother had died, and I had inherited two hundred dollars. When my friend Jen invited me to go from London to Switzerland with her to hear the lectures of an Indian teacher, Krishnamurti, I accepted readily. I had some trepidation about traveling alone and being on my own so far from home, but I knew that it could only help me to become independent.

Camping out in tents, being awakened by cowbells, and sneaking into campsites for showers was an adventure. Jen, her older brother, and I journeyed from spot to spot, cooking vegetarian meals, reading and writing letters, waiting for the conference to begin. People from all over the world gathered to hear the talks of the revered white-haired Indian man. We sat cross-legged on the floor or in stiff-backed chairs and listened as he softly but firmly articulated his beliefs. He was a slight man with thin, expressive hands. He usually wore a white close-fitting shirt and khaki pants. The audience was silent, except for the last day when we were allowed to ask questions. I listened in awe to a theory of life I had never heard about before. He talked about true creativity, development of the self, and the rejection of false doctrines or gods. He himself had been looked to as the new messiah in India, but he had eschewed that role in order merely *to teach*. I realized that for me to accept this man's credo, I would have to reshape my entire life. I was not prepared to do that, so I took in what I felt applied to me and set the rest aside for later consideration.

I missed my family that summer, but only insofar as I needed their reassurance and love. My mother supplied that in her letters; she wrote often and managed to comfort me from afar. Her book had just come out and she was asked to appear on talk shows and travel around the country. She kept me up to date about the Democratic convention, McGovern's successes, and the "tragedy," as she put it, of "the Eagleton affair." She proudly told me about Abigail's acting class and how Abby had gone in to see my father and Carol several times that summer. In one of the last letters my mother wrote me that month, she said:

August 1
Abigail's final production is Thursday night and
she invited Dad up and of course that's alright
and I don't mind him but Carol is not my cup of
tea and I have to be honest. . . . But it's all part of
the game and I'll be wonderful as usual . . .

I felt a guilty sense of freedom at not being involved
in the developments of my family. I was only able to
create an emotional separation from them when there
was a physical distance between us. I worried about
my sister, however, because I did not want her to be
lonely or a silent sufferer. With regard to a problem I
had written my mother about, she responded,

What I appreciated most about that letter was
that you worked on the situation just by writing
about it and talking aloud on paper . . . I just think
that helps so much . . . to get to the feelings that
you may be blocking without realizing it . . . I
worry about Abigail in this regard because I don't
think she trains herself to do this. I think maybe
we both should start writing to her at home and
insist on responses so she can get involved in
what she is feeling. She still has those dreams and
I know she worries about things she can't talk
about.

I received one letter from Carol that summer.
Covering the envelope were little stickers with which
a preteenager might decorate her correspondence: a

dog with floppy ears, a duck saying the words "Did YOU Laugh Today?" a dove of peace with a heart around it, a bird singing "Have a HAPPY DAY!" and an Orville Wright plane trailing the sign AIR MAIL. Her letter began "Hi Ho Hulie," with a yellow smile sticker pasted next to my name. She recorded the events of the past week: her trip to the hairdresser, getting herself "made all blond again," the scalding weather and subsequent purchase of an air conditioner, Abigail's visit and the barbecued chicken dinner they ate. She signed it, "We miss you and love you, Dad and Carol xo." Then she listed the three cats' names and completed her epistle with a sticker of a duck surrounded by hearts. She meant well, I knew that, and she was making an effort to be nice. But I still could not understand what my father saw in her. In any event, I did not think about them at great length while I was away. I returned home changed, less solitary.

# 17

The next year was the most difficult I had experienced since the divorce. I felt estranged from my father and Carol, and the times I spent with them were strained and tense. Because I did not respect Carol, and my father loved her, I could not respect him. For the first five months of my junior year in high school I was more disillusioned by my father than ever before. He was stubborn and defensive. He absented himself from my life at a time when I needed him most.

I kept two journals that fall, one for myself and one as part of a requirement for English class. During this time there was no question as to the reasons for my depression; I could see the most obvious ones myself.

(class)
> September 13, 1972
> Right now I'm thinking about how a

father, or the lack of one, has shaped me and cultivated my feelings about men— or how my feelings toward a man will be when the time comes. After writing that, I don't feel like thinking about it anymore.

(class)

October 12, 1972
I am glad that Mom put in her will that we would live with Grandma and Grandpa if she died because I wouldn't or couldn't stand to live with Carol. I think that if she had a child of her own she would perfect it into a mannerly suppressed person—and I refuse to be suppressed. My life-style is free and my own and not left open to discussion by her. After living with Dad for a year or so, she has superficially adapted many analytical tactics, and I refuse to be an-alyzed by her. Her main fault, I think, is pure gall. I have so much hostility toward her sometimes.

(mine)

October 23, 1972
We spent three days in New York. Saturday and Sunday at Dad's in a sti-fling repressed atmosphere ...

on saturday morning
i sat on a wall

and fell into a
sugary relationship
where i couldn't eat
as i pleased or
leave my apple core
to brown in the
shiny ashtray
now monday night
i am trying to
pull myself together
again.

I wrote the poem as a means of expressing my frustration with Carol's compulsiveness, her desire to have everything "just so." She criticized Abigail for her unwashed appearance, unbrushed hair, and most aggravating to Carol, her propensity to hum at the dinner table. Carol would have none of it. Her complaints were usually suggestive rather than direct, but I knew what she was trying to say. I tried to place myself beyond her reproach. I was civil to her and sometimes even warm. But I couldn't help feeling it was a charade. Where was my father? How did he fit into all of this? He seemed oblivious. Carol called him Daddy (I had stopped long before) and he didn't object. For Christmas one year she gave him a large orange bath towel with Big Daddy embroidered on it in white script.

In my high school that year, the human relations department had organized a series of groups made up of students, teachers, and parents to discuss whatever problems they were experiencing at the time. I had joined one, hoping for an outlet for some of my confusion.

(mine)
> November 2, 1972
> Tonight I feel pain. I feel somewhat lost and like a cold, inapproachable person. I feel lonely, which is a different kind of feeling than previously. Even though I have friends, I don't really feel for them, nor them for me. I want to feel loved, but I don't avail myself.

(mine)
> November 6, 1972
> On Friday in the group, everyone cried —I was in the center at one point. D. understood me. And I think he might perceive how I feel about needing a real father. That word *real* hurts, but sometimes I wonder . . .

Soon after this entry in my journal, my mother was asked to write a series of articles on a children's surgical hospital in Saigon. There was still a wartime atmosphere in Vietnam, but arrangements had been made for her to stay with Americans—reporters or doctors—stationed there. My mother left and for the first time she was away for Thanksgiving. While she was away, the most volatile and painful letters passed between my father and me.

Nov. 7, 1972
5:27 P.M.

Dear Dad,

This has been coming on for a long time, but I didn't want to bother you. I know that you have been having a lot of problems with Gloria, and I don't want to add to your troubles. But I just felt that I had to tell you, and writing seems like a good introduction.

You probably have guessed that I am not getting on very well with Carol. We rub each other the wrong way—she insults Abigail and me each time we come. You had left the table one night when Carol started analyzing me and said how she could understand why Gloria hadn't been able to accept us. Carol is so different from me in her morals, values, and attitudes. If she loves you, as I know she does, maybe I should try to overlook the things that irritate me. I do try but it's getting to the point where I really don't enjoy coming in to see you. I don't want to put words in Abigail's mouth, but I know she feels the same way.

You know, I think I love you, but I don't love Carol and never will. It makes me depressed to come sometimes, and I'm sorry.

Maybe this letter sounds very self-centered, but I don't know how else to put it. I am very confused and feel as if I am hurting you.

Please respond because I want to know how you feel.

>                Love,
>                Julie

After I sent this letter to my father, he did not call or write for three weeks. These were the three weeks that my mother was in Vietnam. It seemed like forever. I knew he was punishing me, giving me the silent treatment he had given others who had offended him. But I'm his *daughter*, I thought. I'm only sixteen years old. While waiting to hear from him, I wrote a great deal in my journal.

(mine)

>   Nov. 13, 1972
>   It always hurts to think that my father is a useless image. We are not connected by recurring love but by a stale reinforcement of the past. I don't know why I feel it so much more now. I don't know why I feel I need it so badly. More right now than ever before. Maybe if I wrote to [my brother] David it would help.

(class)

>   Nov. 19, 1972
>   5:00
>   I don't know how to deal with the feelings I'm having and am feeling more

lost because of it. Right now my father is acting very immaturely. He is waiting for me to give in and call. Or else I upset him so much he can't handle talking to me. Or he is trying to hurt me very badly.

I miss the presence of a man around here more than I can explain. At least when Michael was here with Mom there was some contact. But now there is no one and I am getting colder and colder and going further into myself. Some people have reacted but I don't know quite why. One of the main things, I guess, is that I need one person to really talk to, and I am not getting it.

(mine)

Nov. 26, 1972
It is Sunday and Thanksgiving [with my grandparents] is over. Mom called Friday night and she sounded good.

Where am I? I guess I did hide myself all weekend. That always happens but I never realized it until just now.

I wish I knew where Dad was. What's going on in his mind? Does he hate me?


A few days after this entry in my journal, a letter from my father arrived. As I read it, I cried, blurring the blue ink and spotting the pages.

11/26/72

Dear Julie,

I haven't answered your letter until now because I wanted to get past the immediate impact and not respond quite so emotionally. I think we have needed time away from each other to get a fresh perspective.

First, I must tell you it deeply distresses me that you need to use Abigail for support. If you "don't want to put words in Abigail's mouth" —then why do you do it? It's unfair and dirty fighting. If you are taking a position based on your feelings—then at least have the courage to stand or fall based on your own feelings. That part hurt more than any of the other things you wrote. . . .

That you and Carol are different in many ways is, of course, true. Whether your feeling about Carol is the real issue that's involved or not—I'm not sure. I always love you deeply—but most of the time I experience you as moody, sullen, irritable, and condescending in your attitude. There seems to be so much going on internally— anger, perhaps rage, conflict, and so very much sadness—it's difficult to reach you.

. . . I confess I am at a loss as to . . . how to get to the Julie I believe I know you to be—a warm, loving, sensitive, deep, and good human being. For some reason, it's so difficult for you to talk with me about this—as I so much want to. I know that the last year and a half have been extremely difficult for all of us. I haven't had real peace of mind at any time. . . .

Obviously we can't leave things the way they are now—and have no relationship. Certainly much more honest, open, and direct communication would be far better than what has been. You, of course, have to determine your own feelings, taking into consideration how both Carol and I feel (and we are a unit—who love each other—as well as you and Abigail). . . . People don't have to be alike in all their values to have a loving relationship if everyone is motivated—what is essential is that everyone <u>work</u> at it: bend more, give more, and talk things out.

I'll wait to hear from you.

Love,
Dad

Enclosed with this letter was a note to Abigail in which he apprised her of my speaking for her and reproached her for not telling him how she felt herself. He wrote: "Your relationship with me and Carol does not depend on Julie . . . Love, Dad (+Carol)." I sensed that he was attempting to turn my sister against me.

My father's letter upset me, but I was relieved to have some response from him. I found that I was not afraid to tell him how I really felt.

Nov. 28, 1972

Dear Dad,

First of all, let me say that I do not need Abigail for support and never even thought of "using" her. I don't need anyone to back me up in my thinking. I said that because I knew she would never say it on her own; she very rarely tells anyone her true feelings, and I thought it ridiculous for us to keep up a facade when we were both uncomfortable and hurting. . . .

As to me, I know that I am hard to get along with, but why is it that I get along with other people? It is obviously a combination of me and Carol. As to me and you, I have many deep-rooted feelings about you that I don't even acknowledge and so it is hard for me to relate to you. You don't know me, and if you did, I doubt you would like me. I know that different types of people can get along and love each other, but sometimes they are both just acting and playing a game. I refuse to play those games anymore. If that means not seeing you, then I don't know what to do. I can't help feeling that it is Carol, and not you, that I am reacting to.

I feel like I could love you, because I want to love you. You are my father. But I don't want to love Carol because it would never be real—always artificial.

I know you and Carol love each other, but in my present condition, I don't fit into your unit and don't really want to.

Where am I now?

Oh, well, what is there to say?

Love,<br>Julie

Just about the time that I began working on the problems with my father, my mother returned from Saigon. At last I felt there was someone behind me, who, in spite of any past difficulties, loved me unreservedly. That was one thing I had learned from my mother; she would always "be there" for me, no matter what. With my father it was a constant struggle. And in me two forces pulled at each other: I felt both forgiving and punitive. Had my mother been right about him all these years? Had he really neglected us? I was not prepared to try to empathize with my father. He was the parent who was supposed to know how to treat his children in difficult situations. I wanted him to take charge, but free from wounded pride.

(class)

> January 14, 1973
> Yesterday my father, Carol, Abigail, and I had a group session for a couple of hours. We hadn't seen them for over two months, almost three. Dad took a lot of the blame on himself and said that he realizes that he has been "remiss" for the past five years. Well, we'll just have to start with a strong foundation this time and then start building. Last time, there was no foundation, and we were laying down the bricks on top of nothing. And they just fell through. . . .

Divorce breeds loyalties and disloyal-
ties. Maybe I shouldn't get married so
that I'll never have to get divorced. But
who knows what I'll do tomorrow.

The closing note on this particular episode arrived
in the mail a few days later. The worst was over. I
realized that my attitude may have been harsh, but
I knew that my father was the one who really needed
to change. Only he could pick up the phone and call
us, only he could reinstate himself into our lives in a
more meaningful way. His new optimism read:

1/16/73

Dear Julie,
Naturally it was wonderful to see you and
Abigail, but to be able to share our feelings as we
did—well—that's the greatest! There's no reason
why we can't build a beautiful and mature father-
daughter relationship—and I know I want it.
Please believe what I said—that what I can see and
understand I can cope with—whether I like it or
not. . . .
I have always known the person you are inside,
Julie—and all I can say is—let her out in the open
(I don't mean be a screaming extrovert) but
rather share you with me and us. You have much
beauty in you and I love you dearly. . . . I am
very happy about us and our future.
                                        Love,
                                        Dad

# 18

There was a period of calm after this. I returned to my schoolwork, writing research papers on Sacco and Vanzetti and John Brown, continuing with my Spanish and studying French. In February I borrowed two hundred dollars from a close friend of my mother's and once again went to London with the drama group. There is no mention of my father or Carol in my journal for the next three months, and my mother and I got along well. It seemed that I had temporarily recuperated from the "family disease," and I was immersed in my own life. I found that this was the time I had to work hardest in school if I wanted to go to a good college. I was happier (admittedly a relative term) than I had been in a long while.

Sometime in these quiet months my father and Carol

split up. I didn't know if it was the result of one large falling out or if it had been coming on for some time. Whatever the reason, my father was the one to request the separation; he asked Carol to move out. I was not sorry to see her go, although it surprised me that after the uproar of the preceding months my father was so quick to release the "love" he had just defended so ardently. At least this time there was no alimony to pay, no books and records to fight over. Carol packed her bags, took two cats, and returned to California. I have not seen her since.

May 6, 1973
Dad is alone, and I feel better for him and us. We talked about things—the first father-daughter talk in a long long time. It's funny how I respect him more as a person now.

My father made plans to drive through England and Scotland with Abigail and me for the month of August—for the first time alone. It was the beginning of a new era in our relationship. It was as though he had been on a long vacation and he was finally ready to participate in our lives again. But by this time I was no longer quite as needful. Three weeks before school was out I began seeing Adam, a senior who was going to college in the fall. He was tall and gentle, a basketball player who wanted to be an architect. It was the first time I thought I was in love with somebody, and we had no time to find out. I told my father I needed to return home early from our trip because I wanted

to spend the last few days of summer with my boy-
friend. My father said he understood—hadn't he always said, "Put your love life first"?

Our trip was quite an experience, with my father
driving on the right side of the car on the left side of
the road, something he had never done before. I was
terrified at first, because it was the only time I had
ever seen him not totally in control. The three of us
often slept in one room as we passed through the old
hotels of Bath, Oxford, Stratford-on-Avon, and Edinburgh. My father yelled at Abby about her table
manners; she loved to eat with her fingers, pick her
teeth at the table, and cut around undesirable spots
on her meat and eggs. I got a kick out of the way she
ate and came to her defense, but my father didn't
think it was funny. Abigail still had screaming episodes
at night, and this time she had two comforters instead
of one. We had a good time with our father; he
treated us like queens.

I noticed that he was involved in a correspondence
with a woman in New York. He wrote to her every
couple of days and told us about her. He had met her
in May, and for the first time, he said, he had found
someone who "spoke his own language." Nina was a
social worker in her late twenties. Abigail had met her
at the airport before leaving for Europe, but I had
been unable to make this meeting, so I didn't know
what to expect; my father told me that I would meet
Nina soon.

Anxious to return home, I left from Edinburgh. My
father and Abigail continued driving north. When

they reached Aberdeen, they followed me home. The trip had been a success.

I spent my final year in high school preparing for college. I sent in my applications, had interviews, and completed my requirements as a senior. My mother was very helpful during this time, and my father signed the necessary forms. I had a job in a bookstore, and Adam and I wrote and visited each other when we could.

My mother had met a man on one of her trips to France; they had sat next to each other on the plane. Jerry lived in California. He and my mother began writing and calling each other frequently. My mother sounded more serious about him than she had about anybody for a long time. She had often spoken to me about her loneliness; my role was one of daughter, friend, and confidante. I am sure there is much she did not discuss with me, but we talked openly. I believe she saw Jerry as a hope for happiness.

Thanksgiving came and went, and once again, I did not spend it with my father. Every year this dilemma arose, but I assumed it as a given that I would celebrate most holidays with my mother and sister. Sometime in the fall Nina had moved in with my father and the two of them spent Thanksgiving with her parents. In a letter my father wrote me he said, "Missed you and Abigail *very much*—and always wonder—what do I have to do or be to see you on Thanksgiving—maybe someday . . ."

In this time of renewed communication between

my father and me, I turned to him for advice. He participated in my life from a distance, but I did not feel the same sense of separation. In the same letter he wrote:

Nov. 30, 1973

I'm truly happy that I was able to be there for you when you needed me to be. Somehow it makes me feel that you and I are beginning to develop an understanding of who we are as people—who love each other deeply as father and daughter without the <u>necessity</u> of seeing each other often. I believe it's not the way we would <u>choose</u> to have our relationship, but that's the way it is for <u>now</u>. . . .

I love you—I miss you—I am happy, very happy. You and Abigail would make it complete.

Dad

Knowing that my father and Nina were happy gave me great comfort. It also gave me a sense of stability. I had met Nina and felt that my father had found his match. She helped him to let go of some of his compulsive habits, and most importantly, to take care of his children, to be accessible to us in a way he hadn't been in a long time. She may not have realized the burden she had taken on with the four of us, each struggling in our own way to have some kind of relationship with our father. The relationship required work, trust, and understanding. We had a long way to go.

In May of that year, Jerry came to our house for a

visit. The first thing I noticed about him was his white shoes. *California*, I thought. Then I saw his fine small hands and easy smile. "You're much better looking in person than in your pictures," he said.

Embarrassed, I said, "Thanks," and that was our introduction.

This was the first man my mother had brought home since Michael. I knew that she went out with other men, but I had become used to her alone. Even though I wanted her to be happy, it was an adjustment for me to see her with somebody. She acted differently when Jerry was around, and I felt she was not there only for us. My mother had told me that her work, her writing, was extremely important to her, but that her life would never be complete unless there was a man to share it with. She believed in women fulfilling themselves, but she never once underestimated the necessity of love. Although she seemed ambivalent about Jerry, she wanted to give it a try.

I was accepted by Princeton and spent my last spring at 32 North Sylvan Road. Adam and I had broken up, and high school had lost its challenge long before; I just wanted to finish and move on. We were going to rent the house for the summer, so I truly felt a sense of ending.

As though to reinforce this to myself, I went down into the basement and searched through all of the old moldy boxes I could find. I hit a gold mine when I came upon an entire box of my mother's and father's love letters. They were so passionate and young! My mother's were full of adoration and optimism. I felt strange reading them, as though I were picking over the belongings of dead people. Then I sat on the hills in the backyard, the ones my father and I used to roll down, and let the memories come to me. I remembered the time Abby and I had gone sledding there: we had crashed into a tree and the breath was knocked out of me. I sat on the old, rusty swings which creaked ferociously, lurching the metal swing set out of the ground. There had been so many birthday parties around these swings: girls with ringlets and velvet dresses playing Pin the Tail on the Donkey and Ring Around the Rosy; Abby with her little legs in white tights, her hair, as always, falling in her eyes; my mother in wing-tipped glasses; Steven and David with crew cuts and ties; Uncle Danny, my mother's younger brother, playing the piano in the living room, improvising a hundred variations of "Heart and Soul." On the outdoor porch an old barbecue sat, blackened with charcoal from our summer nights of steak, corn on the cob, and salad. There were no traces of the hopscotch squares we had drawn in chalk. Interrupting the reverie, Smokey came and put her lovely face in my lap. I rubbed her fat belly and her rear leg moved in and out, involuntarily, like a fiddler's wayward arm.

# 19

One issue arising as a result of divorce, causing many angry scenes, is the distribution of money among the family. I rarely discussed money with my father, although I knew my mother's feelings on the matter: she believed she was entitled to more money as both the cost of living and my father's income increased. His first wife had remarried (although not until 1969), and he was still obligated to pay alimony and child support to my mother and alimony to Gloria. When the subject of my college tuition was brought up, my mother found that there was nothing in the divorce contract which stipulated that my father had to contribute. We assumed that my father would offer to pay half. This was not the case.

I remember one hellish weekend in July a month after my graduation, on the telephone with my father, begging him to help pay. I felt a bit guilty, for

Grandma Sallie had died three weeks before, after several years in a nursing home, senile and in pain. She had not recognized us for months.

The tuition was very expensive, and my mother could not afford the entire cost. Indeed, at that point she could not easily put together her half and asked my grandfather to lend it to her. He consented and sent in the checks for two years. Because my mother had quit her job at the newspaper in order to write full-time, my father complained, "Your mother has chosen her means of making a living. I should not be responsible for her choices." My grandfather was stunned that my father would even put up an argument about it; he maligned my father in front of me, telling me what a selfish man he was. I hated it when my grandfather criticized my father. I was furious and embarrassed by the entire situation.

For some reason, my father had never assumed that he would pay half. Perhaps he felt that included in his alimony and child support check were ample funds for a college tuition. Maybe by withholding his money he felt he had some kind of leverage over my mother.

Crying on the phone, feeling humiliated, I persuaded him. My mother took it one step further and had her lawyer draw up papers stating that my father would pay half of my tuition every year for four years and similarly for Abigail when the time came. Now I believe that my father would not question his role as educator/financial guardian. But there was a stubborn streak of pride in him then which would not allow him to accept the responsibility.

Up to this point, my mother had always been the

one to argue with my father about financial matters concerning my life. But from now on it was up to me.

Two weeks after I arrived at Princeton, Smokey died. She had gallstones, and the vet had removed one the size of a tennis ball from her stomach. This was the first sign of her gradual decline; my mother and Abby took her back to the vet and she died there in her sleep. She had been the proud matriarch, presiding on our front porch, greeting all cars that drove through our horseshoe driveway. I had fallen asleep many nights with her weight crushing my legs. In the mornings her wet tongue awakened me on the cheek. Smokey *was* us; she was all the love and crazy affection that lived in our house. When she died a connection with the past was severed. To this day I have not been able to love any animal in the same way.

September 15, 1974
It's really the end of an era. As Smokey dies, so dies my childhood, my school and home days. The end of our happy triangle and I become a point. A single point on my own. . . . Her death has affected me. It is so symbolic—(1) of the end, and (2) of my neglecting her and others.

When I came home for my eighteenth birthday the following week, I expected Smokey to be sitting on the porch, to run over to me and lift her paws up onto my stomach. At night I waited for the metal tags around her neck to jingle, for her bark to let us know that she was guarding our house. Instead there was a great silence.

Smokey's death was the first in a series of changes. I had left home and our "happy triangle," as I put it, was reduced to my mother and Abigail. My mother wrote in one of the many letters I received from her that year: "I do miss you. It's very odd indeed here without you, your room strangely barren. Even going to the store is different—I don't buy yogurt, no green apples—another way of thinking. . . ."

The night they had dropped me off at school for the first time, we all cried; we held on to every minute. It was more than growing up and going to college. I felt I was losing my moorings, my strength. I was afraid that Abby would forget about me: who would take care of her, who would make her tuna sandwiches with just the right amount of mayonnaise and relish, who would scare away the demons in the middle of the night? It was an odd sensation to confront change so directly, to hold on to the present and release it slowly and gently until it flowed backward to become the past. Yet my departure was the first necessary step. As an abbreviated family we had clung to each other, but it was time to love from a distance. It was time to let others in.

One night at school I had a conversation with a new friend. We had just returned from a concert and were sitting in his room, talking. I told him I had a premonition of dying young. I was sure that I would be killed in a car accident before I reached twenty-one. I could not picture myself old, I said. He looked horrified, but he let me go on. I said that if I lived to bear children I didn't want to have any sons. Only daughters, for boys were foreign and strange. I couldn't imagine bringing them up. Finally I told him that I didn't believe two people could ever love each other for fifty years—forget fifty, twenty-five seemed incomprehensible. My vision of love between a man and a woman was one of impermanence. I knew that love between friends, between mother and daughter, between sisters was possible, for I put all my faith and effort into those relationships. Except for my grandparents, who were approaching their fiftieth wedding anniversary, I had not known this lasting love. I believed my own relationships would last only until someone else appeared in my life. My friend had tears in his eyes; he looked upset and perplexed and didn't know what to say. I told him not to worry. I left his room at 3:00 A.M. and returned to my dorm across the courtyard.

Throughout my first year at Princeton the idiosyncrasies and depressions I had accumulated over the years began to break apart. Like melting ice on a pond, large chunks of problems were worked through and floated away from me. I didn't know how much of what I had been feeling emanated directly from the divorce and its aftermath, but I believed that all of my feelings were at least indirectly related.

As soon as I arrived at Princeton, my father was able to approach me on "neutral territory." It was a new place, with no past associations, and my father did not have to compete with any other relatives for my attention. He no longer had to confront 32 North Sylvan Road, the house he had loved and left.

October 5 was Parents' Day for freshmen at Princeton, and my father and Nina were going to spend it with me. I made sure my narrow single room off the living room was spotless, and I asked my two roommates to beware, the Dust-Detector would be arriving soon. My dorm faced the tennis courts, and every morning I awakened to the syncopated rhythm of tennis balls; I knew my father would be amused by that. The full branches of a magnolia tree spread pink across my window. I had hung Matisse's *Blue Nude* on my wall. It wasn't a terrific room, but I had seen worse.

It felt wonderful to introduce my father and Nina to my new friends, to walk slowly around the campus which was to be my only real home for the next four years. My father hadn't known who my friends were since the fourth grade; when I used to mention him, he was only a shadowy figure who lived in New York. He made sure everyone knew who he was this time. He was proud of me for being there, I could tell.

My father and Nina both wore slick velvet pants, and he had on a turtleneck with a dangling pendant around his neck. He took me to dinner at the most expensive restaurant in Princeton, where only parents can afford the prices. The room was filled with other freshmen and their overdressed parents.

There was a moment when Nina left her seat to go to the ladies' room. My father and I were left alone for the first time that day. I looked at him seriously, holding my wineglass tightly. Motioning to Nina's back as she climbed the stairs, I asked, "Is this one going to last, Dad?"

He turned to face me, his lips in a faint smile. It was an expression that meant he knew I wanted to know so much more than just if he and Nina would get married, or live together for a long time. Had he finally settled down, found a woman he could work at loving forever, had he stopped sending me up and down the stairs of his *search*? Could I accept this love as a given in his life and not have to worry about adjusting to new women every few years, new children? Were the repercussions of the divorce which had occurred eight years ago finally over?

"I think so, Julie," he said. I don't know if I believed him then. He had told me that he would never marry again, that living together suited his needs perfectly. I wanted very much to believe him.

Three days later I received this letter,

October 8, 1974

Dear Princetonian Class of '78
and "All-Around Camper,"

. . . I can't tell you how many different kinds of feelings I experienced on our day together—but mostly they were all beautiful. Somehow, the fact that I can relate to you freely on another "turf" (other than in Westport) releases me to be more myself—and not have the feelings of a continuous "uphill" struggle. In other words, it is strictly up to <u>you and me</u> to make a good father and daughter relationship—I wonder if you had any feelings like that. . . .

In spite of its boating shoes and LaCoste shirts, its tennis matches and eating club formality, Princeton turned out to be an important place for me. This was primarily because of the people I met, the emergence of male friendships which I had never had, and the physical distance from my family which allowed me to develop a healthy emotional distance. I looked at my freshman year as the beginning of the "end of the disease." I learned to laugh. I found that I loved to laugh, to shed the serious image I had hidden behind in high school. I had to make up for lost time. There had been so much fun I had missed out on in my unhappiness. The year had its awkward, adjusting moments, but put in a new context, they weren't as devastating as before.

For the first time in many years, I found what can genuinely be called a best friend, Nan. She was from Westport, too, but we had not known each other well in high school. Once at Princeton, when we saw that we both had *Charlotte's Web* and *Harriet the Spy* in our book collections, we became instant friends.

Nan wanted to be an actress: she could recite every one of Dorothy's speeches in *The Wizard of Oz* and sing all the songs from *Funny Girl*. She loved to give presents and flowers, and she made birthday cakes for all of our friends, decorating the frosting with M & M's and raisins. Both Nan and I snuck scoops of ice cream from the dining hall when we thought no one was looking; we met by the coffee and vanilla canisters several times, our spoons in midair. While we were supposed to be studying for our psychology exams, Nan and I would escape to P. J.'s Pancake House and think about our futures. Strolling down the walkways arm in arm between classes, we would belt out verses of Joni Mitchell or Carole King; people always stared at us, but we didn't mind. Sometimes Princeton was so silent and serious that we would make noise simply to stir up some action.

Nan was the first person I didn't feel guilty talking to about my family. We could discuss anything. She helped me to relax and to *give* instead of focusing in on myself, to see the humor in every situation. Nan was surprisingly like my sister: funny, but with many layers beneath the jokes. And I loved her like a sister, a new addition to my family.

Similarly the groups of friends I made helped to ease the transition from home to college life. Each September, after we had only been at school for a few weeks, they would give me a surprise birthday party. People would pop up from behind chairs like so much toast out of a toaster. I was embarrassed every time: ever since my sixth birthday party when I had hidden under the table as they all came in singing "Happy Birthday to You," I had been flustered around surprises. My friends took over where my family had left off.

Strangely enough, I was one of only a few friends

who came from divorced parents, whereas in my high school the divorce statistics had been extremely high. Now I saw people from twenty-year marriages, parents who still genuinely *liked* each other. My mother and father had worked out a nonrelationship. They rarely spoke. They never discussed old times.

It was at about this time that my mother vacillated between staying in Westport and leaving for California to be closer to Jerry. He couldn't leave his job, and because she was a writer, her schedule was more flexible. Abigail was to go out there with her and start high school in Los Angeles the following September. My mother could not decide. I didn't want them to be so far away, but if this made my mother happy, I would learn to live with a telephone relationship.

Abigail lasted two weeks in the Los Angeles high school; she felt out of place and missed her friends. She wanted to go home. Reluctantly my mother sent her to live with my grandparents in New York. It was a difficult separation for them both, but my mother knew that she had to think of herself now. She would call Abby nightly, write her, and come visit every few months. She had to give California a chance.

Now our triangle had points in three different spots on the map: Los Angeles, Princeton, and New York. It was one of the best things that could have happened to us; it gave each of us that gentle shove into independence.

# 20

My parents may not have liked each other, but through it all, I always believed that they loved me. It gave me great comfort.

My father wrote:

> November 20, 1974
> I can't begin to tell you how much the feelings of closeness and warmth between us mean to me. You are becoming the marvelous young woman I always believed you could be. I don't mean I think you're perfect—but rather a person who is more and more in touch with herself and facing realities as they present themselves. If I sound like a father who both loves and respects his daughter—you're right—it's true!

And we reached a moment of great reconciliation. He continued, "I'm so glad you're coming on Thanksgiving. Outside of birthdays it's one of the few holidays I really enjoy and seem to need my family to be together."

Yet, even now, having arrived at this level of renewed love, there are times when the original intensity of our separation is brought back to me with the suddenness of a sharp pain. And there is a similar sting, an immediate rush of tears comes to my eyes for the time we have lost.

Whenever I believe that I have thoroughly come to terms with the finality of my parents' divorce, just when I assume that I have finished grieving, a small incident will open up the wound once more. Whenever I see a father holding on to his little girl, smoothing her hair or reaching down for her hand, when she looks lovingly into his face and plays with his scratchy beard, when I see a father walking down the street with his daughter lifted onto his shoulders, her legs in blue Danskin tights bouncing on his chest, some very old and vulnerable feeling stirs in me. I have been in many movie theaters, grateful for the dark as tears stream down my face; when I glance around me, no one else is crying, for these momentary flashes of fathers and daughters pass by them, perhaps unnoticed. I am always caught unaware, but I know I have to allow myself to mourn now for something which can never be recaptured, something which most children take for granted only because it is such a normal part of their existence.

It is the same feeling, to a lesser degree, I experience when I join other people's families at a dinner table, when the father comes home from work: there is a completeness. I don't think it matters how old or mature I become; the child in me will always miss that rounding out of a family.

Sometimes I wonder if that is why my father surrounds himself with pictures of the good times, when we were all together. They are proof that we were a loving unit once; we did exist.

It was not until I went to college that I perceived the true depth of my mother's character. She had never appeared perfect to me—neither of my parents had—because I was forced to see them as fallible human beings from the moment of their divorce. But now I was able to draw a more complete portrait of my mother: the shadows, the light, the despair, and the happiness. I knew that she was not the neatest person in the world, nor the best cook, but she was rich with love. My freshman year she wrote to me:

> I'll tell you how I feel about you. Your soul, and I do not use the word lightly because nobody talks about it anymore and that is their loss because it is the essence of us, the spiritual side of us, all the poetry and breath we have . . . you have it in abundance. So much is in store for you. Yours will be a life full of the intensity you yearn for, whether it be from books or relationships, or feelings or men or loving or examining. Your soul, you see, is rich, full of texture, sweetness, pain.

But embrace what you see a little more than you have. Confront that world out there whether it be the street lights of Princeton, N.J., or a chance conversation. Watching you grow is like seeing a water lily in a pool of water, closed, resting in the morning and by midday open, ready, floating with a rhythm and confidence. And another thing. Write. Forget that your mother writes. Get only the good out of me, the encouragement, the seeds planted for ideas. The courage to put it, whatever it is, on paper. And it will be only your own.

My love for you is never-ending, a long continuous line meeting itself end-to-front only to begin again. My respect increases every day. I take pride in your struggle, have confidence in your courage.

I love you. That's it.

And you know me, a bit crazy in a decent sort of way.

And if you needed me to talk to and I was in California or Tibet, and I had a few dollars in my pocket, you know I'd be on the next plane.

That's the way it is.

Mom

There were times, in spite of everything, when I felt blessed.

# 21

In the spring of my sophomore year, I began spending time with someone I had known fairly well as a freshman, Bobby. We had been in several classes together; we both loved European literature and dance, writing and music. We cared about the Soviet dissidents; since 1974 Bobby had kept a photograph of Vladimir Bukovsky in his room, holding a private vigil for his release. Bobby was a fiery mixture of politician and romantic. When he spoke, he was articulate, impassioned. At night he played his guitar for me with a quiet gentleness. There was an aura of idealism and challenge about him—to everything I said he would propose a list of reasons why it could not be so. His self-assurance prompted me to contradict him constantly.

It disturbed Bobby that I was pessimistic about the

endurance of love. With the same resolve as he would tackle a difficult problem, he was determined to persuade me that regardless of what my parents had been through, I could still maintain a relationship, that love could last.

He would come to my room early in the morning, stretching a handful of lilies of the valley under my nose to wake me up. Or when I was studying for an art history exam he would appear at my window with raspberries, insisting that the light was just right for a bike ride to the grad college. We would take the bus to New York and go to the ballet and concerts in the Village. Instead of writing our term papers we would sit on the steps of the Metropolitan Museum, eating Creamsicles and applauding the jugglers and mimes.

When school was out, I worked as a counselor in a French camp. At the end of August, Bobby joined me in Nice for a three-week trip. On a whim we took the midnight ferry to Corsica, arriving just as the sun rose pink over the island. We returned to Paris before driving through the châteaux country in the Loire Valley. He showed me the places he loved, the woods at Chenonceaux, a special restaurant in Amboise. Through the course of our travels, we laid out our pasts like so much food on a picnic table. We talked about my parents' divorce. He listened; he insisted that *my* life could be different.

Just as he was willful, he was playful and vital. He was like a little boy running all over the house, leaving a trail of socks and pencils. He wanted to know how everything worked; he wished he could be an astronaut. His spontaneity, so threatening at first, was wonderfully contagious. I felt like he had thrown a bucket of water over me and washed me clean. By the end of our trip I knew that for the first time I was truly happy. I loved him.

One day in May at the end of my sophomore year, I was sitting outside eating lunch with some friends. We were opening our mail, laughing and enjoying spring, looking forward to the end of school. I opened a letter from my mother, sealed in an envelope addressed in her usual illegible handwriting with an upside-down stamp in the corner. I told my friends that my mother had never put on a stamp upright in her life, and they were amused.

This letter was different from her other ones. She had sold our house, she wrote, and the deal was final. The new people were to move in in September, so she would have the summer to pack up, put the furniture in storage, and have the house thoroughly cleaned.

I was stunned. I started to cry and I felt their silence around me. Apologizing for crying, I left the table to go to my room.

I could not imagine never entering my house again. I could not envision other people living in the air and rooms and smells that were us. Of course it had become too big for just my mother and Abigail; they rattled around in it like peas in a barrel. I knew that my mother had outgrown Westport; she had utilized all the resources it could give her and met every available single man there. She probably should have left the town long before. But to lose our house was to lose a *home*. I knew no other. In spite of the unhappiness I had often known there I loved too deeply the life we had created in those rooms.

Houses are resilient, much more so than people. This house had witnessed the fighting between my parents, my father's departure in his maroon Buick Skylark; it had nurtured me through high school, given up its faithful sentry, Smokey, and welcomed my eighteen-year-old independence. And although the paint peeled in places and weeds climbed the gutter pipes, even though the basement flooded after every rain and the heat clanged on winter nights like angry spirits demanding attention, the structure still stood, proud and parental, for it had housed a family once.

In the time that has passed since my mother moved from Westport, I have never stopped grieving for that house—for the memories which can now only float with no rooms in which to enclose them, for the home where I lived a childhood with my father and mother, my two brothers, and my little sister. I often have dreams about that house. I remember every corner, each creak it made in the middle of the night when no one was walking on the old wooden floors. My life, in letters, papers, and clothes, has been packed away in boxes and stored in the closets of my grandparents' house in New York, and my books lie in the garage of my father's house in the country.

There is an ache in me for that home, a place where a family, no matter what its makeup or size, could live from time to time. A place to return to, to welcome guests in, a yard to wander in and think about old times.

One day last year I went back to Westport and drove through the horseshoe driveway. The people who live there had redone the roof, repainted the house, and cuticled the landscaping. The once-grand house looked small and inconsequential now. There was nothing to remind me of us. They had even filled in the hole in the gravel driveway where, every spring, a large puddle used to form and last throughout the summer.

There was a turning point in the lives of our family which was so simple, so long overdue, that I wondered why my mother and father had never thought of it before. It was the last week in January of 1977 and I was spending the intercession vacation in Cape Cod with Bobby and his two roommates. The day had been blustery as we had forced our way against the wind in the dunes, shouting to each other above the noise of the waves. When we arrived back at the house, my mother was on the phone, calling from New York.

"I have something to tell you," she said. Her voice was light.

"What, Ma?" I asked.

"Well, your father and I had lunch today and we had a very good talk. It's the first time I've just sat down with him face-to-face in such a long time."

"How many glasses of wine did you need?" I interrupted.

She laughed. "Only two. But listen, we really *talked*. He made sense. For once both of us weren't so defensive. I stopped criticizing him for the past and he left his big ego out of the conversation. What I mean is, I think we can be *friends* now. I just thought you might like to know."

"That's wonderful!!" I shouted into the phone. "You didn't slam any doors, he didn't hang up on you when you made the arrangements?"

"Nope. Look, I'm not saying that we're best friends. The thing is, we have finally reached the point where we can discuss you and Abigail without screaming at each other. You two are the only things we have in common anymore. And you know I've always wanted you and Ab to have a good relationship with your father. Anyway, it was very nice and the next time I'm in New York I'll call him again. It's such a relief."

"Mom, I'm *so* glad. I can't tell you how happy it makes me."

"You know, I think Nina must be having a good effect on him."

"I know she is. But also, maybe it's just *time*. You've changed too, Ma."

"That's certainly true. As long as I don't mention the word *lawyer* or *money*, I'm okay."

We both laughed. "Thanks for calling, Mom. You made my day. You really did."

" 'Bye, I love you."

"Love you too."

When I hung up the phone, I was aware of having

feelings I had never, could never have, had before. The idea that my father and mother might actually be more than coolly cordial to each other, might even like each other again, had been so far removed from the realm of possibility that I had not even considered it. I had not even wished for it because it didn't occur to me that it could happen. I had become accustomed to their inability to talk to each other, their mutual disapproval and distaste; I never imagined they could relate in any other way. This news made me doubly happy, for it was so unexpected. It was small but bounteous progress. I felt comforted, as though a loose and very disturbing thread had finally been tied into the rest of my life's network. I believed there would be an end to the dissonance I felt whenever I thought of my father and mother together. This tension had been present for so long I wondered if one lunch could really alleviate it. I decided to trust in the changes time had brought to my parents.

This lunch turned out to be the breakthrough which simplified many things for the workings of two separate families. It was easier to discuss holidays, feelings were not hurt, and more importantly, there was an absence of the just-hinted-at antagonism which had colored all conversations about the "other parent." My mother and father were still wary of each other, as though they weren't sure what weapon the other might still have ready to brandish. But some spark of vengeance had finally been extinguished.

Since that time there have been small steps toward a

peaceful coexistence between my mother and father (when they are on the same coast). They will never forget why they divorced the other, but they have learned to suppress or to confront these feelings maturely.

In May of that year, Bobby and I performed in the small café at Princeton. He played the guitar and we both sang. I invited my mother and Abigail, my father and Nina. It was to be the first time my whole family would be assembled in one room, at one small table lit by a candle. The other tables were filled with friends. For me it was a milestone. As I sang I saw them looking proudly at me, my mother crying a bit, as she always did. Never having mastered mechanical objects, she fiddled with her tape recorder, erasing the first half of the concert as she taped the second. Before the last song, I announced that it was a special night because my family was together for the first time in ten years. I dedicated the song to them. I sang the lullaby my mother used to sing to me when I was a little girl before Abigail was born: "I Gave My Love a Cherry." There was no accompaniment, only my voice filling the darkened room.

My father sat between my mother and Nina, his face thoughtful, his eyes misty and sentimental; my mother, hidden behind her glasses, sitting straight in her chair, *kvelling*, as they say; and Abigail, whose face never expressed her thoughts, silently crying as she picked at the wax dropping onto the table. When it was over, there was that moment of hesitation, then applause. Exhilarated, I rejoiced privately for the strange combination that was my family.

I had not seen much of my brothers in the preceding couple of years, but I didn't know if this was a function of our odd family relationships or merely because they were older and had gone on to the next stages in their lives. Steven had been graduated from college and moved out to San Francisco, where he met and married his wife in the summer of 1976. David had traveled to Australia and back, lived in upstate New York, and finally settled in Southern California where he was studying for his Ph.D. in psychology. August, 1977, was the date set for his wedding, and the entire family—his mother and stepfather, my father and Nina, Abigail and I, and of course Steven and his wife —were flying out to Los Angeles for the event. I had not been able to go to Steven's wedding because that had been the summer I was in France. So I looked forward to David's wedding as a time for the four "children" and my father to be together. We loved it when this was possible. The last time had been in New York on my eighteenth birthday. There was much catching up to do, rolls of film to fill up, memories to relive.

The wedding ceremony was outside, in the courtyard of a church. There was nothing traditional about it, from my brother's white cowboy shirt, to Susan's peach-colored dress, to the words they had written for their service. The family and a few friends stood around them in a semicircle. Nina and I cried—for different reasons, I'm sure. Abigail looked lovely and slim in a white dress. My father's thick hair was nearly all gray. I couldn't imagine what he was thinking as his oldest child, his firstborn, kissed his Australian bride.

August 22, 1977

Dear Dad,

I want to thank you for the wonderful weekend in California. The fact that we were all together. It really meant a lot to me, as I'm sure it did to you, and I truly felt a sense of family, no matter how many tributaries.

During the ceremony I felt only hope for the future, hope for David's happiness and the longevity of their marriage. It must have been quite a sensation for you to know that you had fathered all of that life there—Steven, David, Abigail, and me. You began the chain, and now we all will begin our own chains of life. It hit me as I listened to the words, heard them speak to each other, saw the love in their eyes. I cried hard, like at your wedding [to Gloria] because it brought up all the pain of before, the attempts at love, the renewed hope, the disappointment. Through it all we will be strong, I feel, we have made it, and I hope now that you are as happy as you can be. We all love you very much.

Dad, thank-yous are not enough, but I think you know what I mean. Most of all, I hope for your happiness, for you to feel stable, complete, and productive. I hope Nina is your happiness; she is a wonderful person.

Much much love, Julie

# 22

The autumn is always beautiful in Princeton. Along every walkway, from every window, all you can see is orange, yellow, and red. With the backdrop of ivy-covered buildings and sharp blue sky, it is a time like no other.

In October of my senior year, my mother told me that she and Jerry were separating. It had been a mutual decision, she said. There was no hostility or bitterness, merely a parting of ways. I had felt from the beginning that although Jerry was encouraging about my mother's writing, he did not quite understand what motivated her. Her eccentric approach did not fit in with his plan of things.

I was worried about my mother living alone. This time she didn't have Abigail and me to come home to. Abigail continued to live in New York, but she decided to spend her senior year in high school with my father and Nina. Abby looked forward to this new living arrangement, the chance to spend more time with our father. My mother began to make a life for herself in Los Angeles.

Senior year at Princeton was a whirlwind for me. My interest in politics increased as I researched my thesis on Jean-Paul Sartre. I became involved with campus politics as I worked closely with a group attempting to abolish the selective eating clubs. With two hundred other students I picketed the administration building daily requesting that the university's trustees divest the stock they had with corporations doing business in South Africa. This issue caught on like no other in my four years at Princeton—I found myself thoroughly absorbed and changed. As June approached, it was a time to prepare to leave my friends, professors, my home. For I *had* found a home to replace the one I had lost.

I was startled to learn that my father and Nina were not getting along. I thought they had passed the trial mark; they had been together almost five years. Nina was very unhappy; she lost weight and appeared fragile. My father, unusually quiet, did not tell me what was happening for a long time. By my graduation, they were virtually separated. I did not blame either of them. Instead I felt deeply sad, overwhelmingly weary. Another divorce of a sort, even though there were no legal papers or lawsuits. I knew I would continue to see Nina, for she had been an important part of my life for five years.

My father tried to spend time alone and with his
male friends. I couldn't look at him as I told him I
didn't want to meet any more of his girl friends. I was
tired of making the effort to know and love them and
then watching them leave our lives. Every time one
of my parents separated I experienced a vicarious pain.
For my own sense of survival, I knew I couldn't do
this forever.

I graduated from college, wearing a black robe and
a red arm band protesting Princeton's continued in-
transigence in the South Africa divestment issue.
There was a lot of kissing good-bye, promising to
write. Bobby and I posed for pictures; Nan and I
hugged each other, already reminiscing. *You can't
hold back the tide*, I thought. *Move on.*

For the last eight years, whenever Abigail and I
have  gone to visit our father, we have slept on the
fold-out couch in the room where my father keeps his
clothes. Except for the short time when Abigail lived
with my father and Nina, and she slept in the tiny
room with the cabinet used to store canned foods, we
have made do with the couch. Sisters can do that—
share a double bed and whisper late into the night.
Whenever Abigail comes home from her college in
Boston on vacation, this is where she returns to, unless
my mother buys her a plane ticket to Los Angeles.

In the short time that my father has been alone,
the three of us have recaptured a familiar pattern. We
are older now, but at times we willingly fall into the
roles which were determined for us before, when we

used to take the train to New York and meet our father at the train station. We all look very different, Abigail having stretched into a narrow-hipped beauty or, as one friend called her, "an exotic Iranian princess." Having lost her bangs and belly long before, she is no longer just a cute and uncombed litle girl. On the contrary, she is the one who knows how to dress in style, which rings and bracelets suit her graceful arms. My father has passed slowly into middle age. The starkness of his youth, his black hair, blue eyes, and thin frame have matured into a softer attractiveness. There are hints of the younger man still in his face. He never wears ties, rarely puts on a jacket. He is fond of turtlenecks and proudly wears the sweat shirts from Abigail's and my alma maters.

We are much more independent now than in the old days. We often make separate plans for the evenings. When we are together, in the mornings we eat bagels and drink coffee in our bathrobes, listening to Stephen Bishop or Phoebe Snow. My father takes us out to dinner, usually to Poletti's on the corner, where we can watch spaghetti being spun out of a machine. He is proud to be with us, and I enjoy seeing him so happy. Over wine he becomes sentimental and tells us how much he loves us. We each squeeze one hand. We don't choose girls for him behind his back anymore; he takes care of that himself. As a matter of fact, this Christmas Abby and I bemusedly helped him to wrap presents for his "women friends." He keeps us informed about the progress of certain relationships.

When you don't have a family in the traditional

sense, you work with whatever combination of relatives you have. On holidays this can be particularly
disconcerting, because there is in me at these times
a yearning to be part of a real family. In spite of the
strength of the love we feel for each other, on holidays
there is always the sense of something missing.

This last Thanksgiving our family was divided between two coasts: my mother and her parents, my
uncles and my brothers in California; Abigail, my
father, and I in New York. The past few Thanksgivings we had gone to Nina's parents' house in Long
Island, but this was no longer possible. The day before
Thanksgiving I felt extremely depressed. Not only
was there to be no turkey, no sweet potatoes baked
with a thick layer of gooey marshmallows, but there
wasn't going to be any large family gathering at all!
My father, Abigail, and I were going to eat a midday
supper at an elegant restaurant. Of course the most
important thing was being together, and it didn't *really*
matter where we ate, but the person in me who is in
many senses of the word a traditionalist felt cheated. I
was not so unhappy at how we planned to spend the
day, but rather angry at the situation which prevented
us from having a large family celebration.

The three of us spent the morning dressing. My
father even wore a jacket for the occasion. We had a
sumptuous meal at the Café des Artistes. We loved
the paintings on the wall and the fresh fruit on the
center table. Never having been to a restaurant on
Thanksgiving before, Abigail and I were fascinated
by the types of people who *do* spend their holidays in

this way. There were Europeans, for whom this was merely a welcome day off, elderly couples with no place to go, out-of-towners who brought their families to a chic New York restaurant, and, at the table next to ours, a middle-aged divorced woman and her two grown daughters. They were nearly our mirror image (the girls should have been boys). All that needed to happen was for my father and the woman to fall madly in love and marry, and then next Thanksgiving we could have our turkey and cranberry sauce at her town house. Though it had television series potential and the woman and my father flirted quite a bit, no proposals were made.

My father was very happy being with his two daughters on Thanksgiving, and I knew how much it meant to him. I still felt let down. It rained that afternoon and the three of us went to see a movie.

After that weekend, my father and I put Abigail on the train for Boston. How many Sunday nights we had spent in train stations! It was odd for me not to be getting on with her, waving good-bye to our father as he made faces at us through the window. This night he surprised us by flashing her the monkey face just as we were about to leave. Abby laughed and motioned him away, loving it.


When Abigail and I spend time with our mother now, it is much more like "coming home." Wherever she is, that is home. Visiting her in Los Angeles, in the apartment furnished with the couches, dressers, and paintings from our house on North Sylvan Road, I am comforted, for the best things of the past have found a place for themselves in the present.

We are, in effect, the nuclear family which has now grown up and moved out on our own. The familiarity we feel with each other, the bonds which hold us comfortably together but do not pull too tightly come from our years as a threesome. Others come and go freely with us now—boyfriends, men and women friends. We were an incomplete family by default; no one would have chosen it that way. That entity we established in those years with no man around the house—that is what defines our family.

I am proud of my mother and my sister. My mother looks younger every year. People assume we are sisters. She is always trim and vivacious. Her beauty has increased with time. She needs less makeup for her youthfulness gives her the impression of having just stepped out of the ocean. She is dark and smaller than I am. She is a professional writer, and now she produces for television. As a mother, she has continually given me love, courage, and compassion, outrage at injustice. How I love her for passing that compassion on to me! Her search for herself, for her own fulfillment, continues—but I know she will always have a space for me.

We talk on the phone for hours (my mother firmly believes that she alone supports the phone company), bringing each other up to date, assessing the latest world crises, commenting on the choices for Pulitzer prizes, laughing about Abigail's sardonic approach to life. For the past few years my mother has been jotting down notes while talking to Abigail on the phone, for her Woody Allen humor and one-liners delight us continually.

I would like my mother to find a man who could keep up with her, who would have her energy, curiosity, depth. He would have to be extremely intelligent, yet unashamedly loving. The difficult part is finding the combination—a person who would understand the temperament of the writer, yet give selflessly, receive love gracefully. In her past relationships, my mother has found one without the other, one side of a color without its complement. I believe she would like to spend the rest of her life with one man.

We talk about what this man would be like and wonder if such an eccentric-beautiful-brilliant-creative-human being exists. Someone who would understand if she holed up in a rented room on Malibu Beach for a month to "get back to herself," to writing, to solitude. Someone who would not expect dinner on the table every night at six, but would cook it by himself or surprise her with delivered Chinese food. A man who would watch old Bette Davis movies on TV until 3:30 in the morning, even if they both had to wake up at eight. Who wouldn't get angry every time she didn't finish a sentence or discussed John Updike before breakfast. I think she may have found him in the man she is seeing now. If my mother were truly happy, fulfilled in work and love, I would know that a final justice had been done, that she had found the best of both worlds.

The times that my mother, sister, and I are together, we relive old patterns: my mother and I make dinner while Abby talks on the phone. I clear the table while Abby watches TV. We keep an eye out for movie stars in Hollywood restaurants; Abby's eyes light up with the briefest glimpse of Nick Nolte's blond hair or her idol Lucille Ball's chauffeured car. Abby still makes fun of my mother, but in a more good-humored way. Being the most well-informed in matters of this nature, Abigail has been dubbed the family fashion consultant. She helps us choose and put together our clothes. A "Yes, it looks good" from her is the seal of approval before walking onto the street. My mother's "jerky foot" driving with stops and starts thirty miles an hour on the freeway makes Abigail nauseous and terrified. She is the one to say "shove over" to my mother and take over at the wheel. My sister keeps us laughing, yet her humor is outdone only by her perception. She has always been the analyst for all of her friends, and on occasion she has been known to give therapy to her friends' mothers. Her medium is the telephone, and she pulls from her eighteen years of experience to give out sound advice. Her wisdom gained early, she makes sense. She is a loving, loyal friend.

As sisters we are a funny team. After so many years of me bossing her around, fending for her, and worrying about her closed-off feelings, she has now come into her own. Her newfound self-sufficiency has made her imaginative and strong. As an older sister, nothing makes me happier than when she calls me to help her with the introduction to a paper on D. H. Lawrence, or how to conjugate irregular French verbs, or what to say to a boy whose attentions she would rather not have. She expresses her feelings much more openly, although there is still a lot of old material inside which has yet to emerge. Abigail still has her nightmares from time to time, and I worry about that.

I continue to love my sister in a way that I don't love anyone else. We have lived through the same battles from the inside; we have been witness to and among the wounded. We join the ranks of the survivors.

# 23

In the years following the divorce, I had neither the foresight nor the wisdom to understand any of what had happened from my father's point of view. I was too busy experiencing my own. Now that the resentment and hurt have worn off and I approach my father as an adult, I see things in a different way.

I have tried to imagine what it must feel like to have a family and a beautiful home, a backyard full of forsythia, and a dog; fires in the winter, sprinklers in the summer, tucking in your children at night, locking all the doors to the outside; being the protector, the man of the house. And then, after gradually building and accumulating this, to suddenly lose it all. Not only to lose a primary love relationship, but the whole package that the marriage had created. No one forced my father to stop loving my mother or to leave. But once gone, I am sure he must have felt a great loss.

A cruel accompaniment to loss must have been guilt—guilt for leaving, for ending our family unit, for uprooting the love in our lives and dispersing it across the state line; guilt for subjecting his two little girls to fighting, bitterness, unhappiness, for depriving us of himself on any regular basis, for not being the kind of father he may have wanted to be.

I am sure he felt anger and frustration because he could no longer live in his house. He has told me many times how painful it was to drive in the driveway when he waited for us to come out, how he missed the Sunday mornings of rich coffee and classical music, the old house enveloping us in its protective arms.

My father has made the decisions which have affected his own life. But I believe there are times when he regrets the way it has turned out. A divorced father does not have an easy time of it, any more than the divorced mother who suddenly has to head a household. The father who doesn't have custody of his children has to be a diviner of thoughts, a transmitter of love from afar. He is expected to continue being a father when his given role is altered; only he can define the new role.

How I wish my father could have known then all that we both know now! If only he could have understood that I needed a relationship with *him*, and not with him *and* the woman he was presently seeing. He always used to say how much it upset him to "play second fiddle" to my mother; I wish he hadn't been so proud and hadn't taken out his anger on Abigail and me.

But I forgive him. Over the last five years I have learned to accept him as he is, to move beyond the past. He has redeemed himself in my eyes. He has been a concerned and caring father. And although I can never recapture my little girl adoration, I love him now, as my father.

I have asked him if he were to live his life over again, what would have been his ideal life. "I would have lived alone from the time I was twenty-one until I was thirty," he said. "Figured out who I was and then gotten married. Had a family. And stayed married."

I wish that had been the way things worked out.


When I look back to determine what I have gained and what I have lost as a child of divorced parents, I believe I relinquished my right to innocence and earned a place closer to my parents' true selves. I lost the image of perfection in exchange for parents as flawed human beings.

I never had to confront the two-on-one situation with my mother and father; they were individuals. I never wrote joint letters or had telephone conversations where the other parent was listening in.

However, their tendency to treat me as an adult at a young age presented me with a set of facts and feelings I did not always want to be aware of. There have been times when it has been easier to shirk these responsibilities of "awareness" and hide behind "I don't want to know." I appear to be very grown-up and able to handle their confidences, but when it becomes too personal, I want to be the child again. Perhaps they believed that if they treated me as an adult, the child's wounds would no longer be capable of stinging.

The other side of this is that in my parents I have two loyal *friends*, people I can turn to at any time, about any problem. I discuss with my mother the same things I would tell my best friend; I believe she thinks of me in the same way. Similarly I trust my father's insights about me. He helps me decipher my dreams; we talk openly, freely.

Even though my mother and father are able to speak to each other now, they have very little in common. Their life-styles are so different, I wonder how they ever lived under the same roof. Strangely enough, in all of these postdivorce years, I have *never* been alone with just the two of them. Since graduation from Princeton, I have gone out to dinner with them and Abigail once, but that is all. As I tend to do, I built up this meeting beforehand, looking for old feelings, trying to find unity in this foursome, and again, I feel disappointed. They can't hold each other's eyes anymore; there is no connection. My mother talks about what she read in the *New York Times* that day; my father's eyes wander toward a pretty waitress. He brings up the names of people; she discusses ideas. Or, as my mother used to say, she talks green, he talks blue. As I sit between them at the dinner table, part of me reaches out to one, part of me to the other. I try to figure out whom I most resemble. Then there is the middle, the core which stands independent of them both, objective and growing.

Although the process of dealing with my parents as divorced, single people is never-ending and the way in which I approach them is unlike that of many of my friends, the time has come to relieve my mother and father of their part in shaping my life and take responsibility for myself. Whatever damage has been done has already taken place. I can no longer blame them for who I am or who I will become. I can only look back at that which has been offered to me, the "tools," as my mother used to say, with which they have suggested I build my life, and choose to incorporate what I need. They have taught me what it is to love—not each other, unfortunately—but how to nurture, expand, and give security to a child. That child, me, has been tossed about, perhaps too much, as my mother and father struggled independently of each other to make new lives for themselves after the divorce. Now I see clearly the mistakes they made, the strengths they developed. And even though I am an adult and one day will, I hope, be a parent, I believe I will always identify with the child whose parents divorce.

We, the children, are the victims of our parents' mistakes. Obviously no father or mother willfully hurts their child when they realize they no longer love each other. But the pain which results from the separation and the "regrouping" is inevitable. People say that children are adaptable; they adjust to new environments and make different friends easily. Children, they say, like tennis balls off a wall, bounce back. They struggle to grow up and because they are so resilient, they survive. I agree—children *are* terrific survivors. What I have experienced is nothing compared to the horrors witnessed by children in concentration camps, from alcoholic families, from extremely poor homes, of battered wives, or from foster homes. I was, in no sense of the word, a "deprived" child. Even those children who have truly suffered, who have never known the love I have felt, continue to live and overcome their pasts. The scars are there, however. I believe that we children feel more than we reveal; we hurt more than we are able to cry; and we perceive the truth of what is happening around us most of the time. Children bounce back because we know no other life than this.

A year ago my uncle and his wife separated after eight years of marriage and a son who was about to celebrate his sixth birthday. My only first cousin, beautiful and blond, lovingly spoiled and wise. As I watched their marriage end, even though the circumstances were entirely different, I felt as though I were reliving something too closely. I found that in spite of my love for my aunt and uncle, I could not speak to them as they waged their war over the future of their child. Why couldn't they foresee what they were doing to him? I wrote in my journal,

January 31, 1978
Another victim. Little boy who knows only that
Daddy and Mommy fight, don't live together, fly

back and forth across the country, depositing him. Happy birthday, little cousin. Six years old and already so confused.

The process will begin—the pain, the exchange of visits, holidays, two birthdays, two Christmases, the double life. Nothing will ever be normal again—the break, the splintering, the turning point. How I wish I could save you from the hurt you will know, the loss you will feel. The loss of the family: no, the <u>death</u> of the family. The beginning of the new life, the strange and unfamiliar pattern of Mommy or Daddy—Mommy with other men, Daddy with other women. There's no road back to normalcy, ever. . . . We <u>are</u> the passed-around generation. . . . <u>Let me never make a victim of a child of mine</u>. . . .

I use them as an example because I felt for the three of them so strongly, and I witnessed the distintegration of their love. Although this love-turned-bitter saddened me greatly, I knew the "adults" would both eventually recover. I worried about my cousin, how he would come to view his parents, how they would each turn him against the other, fill his head with the wrongdoings of the other, if they would allow him to love them both equally without "taking sides." I was frightened of the poison that would take his sweet innocence from him. I wanted to warn them how to treat their son, to avoid mistakes and help him grow up healthy and loving. They held this soft, young person in their hands: I thought I could protect him. But they have done what they thought best. He is seven now, less confused, a bit more grown-up. Now he, like me, my sister, and brothers, is a veteran.

When my aunt and uncle separated, my grand-father immediately clipped my aunt out of a family photograph that had held a prestigious spot in their kitchen. Just as he had razored out my father's form from my baby picture, my "evil" aunt disappeared. He filled in the hole with a picture of my cousin. The message was clear—we were to disown her for what she had "done" to their son and their grandson. When I saw this, the anger and the sadness of that which I had seen so many times before burned in me. In my journal I wrote,

> June 20, 1978
> Just as Gloria, Kelly, and Amy have been dis-carded, just as Grandpa has cut Dad and Aunt P. out of pictures on his kitchen wall, we are taught to love and then to expel those who have done us no wrong. Clipping them out of photos as though they had never existed, as though they had had no part in creating our lives.

Throughout my life I have gleaned the meaning of the unspoken credo: there is no greater love than that between blood relatives. You must love the person who is related to you by blood no matter what he does —but the person's love you have acquired through marriage is somehow dispensable. Indeed, loyalty to your blood relative requires you to turn off love for others, to cast them off like shoes you have worn and no longer need.

This rule cannot hold between a child and two parents, however, because the child is related to both by blood. The parents make the break between each other, both physically and legally, but the child does not. The most important issue in this business of divorce, this rending of a family, is how to preserve the child's love in the midst of hate and incompatibility, how to supply the sun and soil, the air and water in which this love can blossom. A child has to learn that although his parents could not sustain love for each other, he has the power to continue to love them both.

A child's love is so simple at first—given freely. The years twist it, tie strings to it, and manipulate it so that it becomes a commodity at our parents' bartering tables.

# 24

When I go to weddings, I am struck by the lavishness of the costumes, the adherence to tradition, and the overwhelming sense of joy. The couple has spent months preparing for this event, from choosing the type of the engraved invitations to the color of the bridesmaids' shoes. The wedding day is to be the most beautiful in a woman's life, the most sacred and symbolic. Beneath all the trappings, it is a commemoration of love. There is so much hope for happinesss that every person is swept up in the optimism.

What frightens me is how soon after the honeymoon the china pattern and silver spoons are forgotten. There may be a glorious fanfare for the day of the union of two people, but after the rice settles the couple must begin to make a life. There seems to be a tremendous imbalance between the high expectations before and the real life afterward.

It strikes me that when we are young, we think we know ourselves and what we will desire from a marriage of a lifetime. Yet when I look at the people of my parents' age, I see that the vows they made twenty-five years ago have not always taken into consideration the changes they themselves would undergo over time. How can people expect to predict the rhythms of their middle age when they are twenty? Yet many people fall into young marriages, anxious for "security," not willing to find out *first* who they are and thereby risk the loss of their potential mate. I worry about women who let men make all their decisions for them, who give up an essential part of themselves when they marry.

I believe that marriage is the most important step two people can take, in the sense that it determines the shape of their individual and joint futures. Even more important and with far-reaching consequences is the decision to have a child. Sometimes I wonder how many couples have children merely to provide themselves with a playmate or a cute baby to make them laugh after a hard day of work. I wonder if they realize that not only do they affect the nature of their own relationship, but they take on total responsibility for the spirit of another human being. I find myself angry when child after child is subjected to the mistakes of their parents' youth and irresponsibility. The effects of the early years of our lives never wear off—indeed, a parent's grip on a child does not necessarily lessen even when we are grown.

The most difficult problem arises when the parents, the motivating force behind the family, begin to move away from each other. Couples who stay together "for the sake of the children" do not solve their marital problems. And, more times than not, children can see through the pretense; the tension is ever-present. The reason that the breakup of a marriage is so devastating to children is that it is the dissolution of the *family*. I don't know that children ever understand the nature of their parents' love for each other to begin with. What they grieve for is not necessarily *that* lost love, but the loss of order and completion—the end of regularity, an atmosphere of togetherness and sharing, and the differences between men and women. The family, the center for comfort and acceptance. becomes instead another place of uncertainty.

I believe that the people of my generation place a high value on personal independence, career, and self-sufficiency. Most women I know, myself included, intend to work for a living. Behind all this I find that there is a desire for an order similar to the one our parents sought: many people will choose to marry, have children, have a house and dogs—they will create a family. The problems I foresee are those of attempting to combine a family and a career. And in spite of the attack which has been leveled against the nuclear family in recent years, I continue to believe it is a constructive and healthy way of organizing a life, a series of lives.

If I compare myself with people my age who have married parents, I see that they are no more perfect than I am, their problems no less complex. The difference may be that they have always assumed that marriage to one person for life is possible or the best way, whereas I have had to work my way through much disillusionment and disappointment to arrive at a similar conclusion. I am still not positive that it is a given for every person. My parents' divorce has made me wary and frightened of the decay of love.

And yet, although it might seem that after all the instability in marriage I have witnessed, I would be pessimistic and resigned to an inevitable finish to love, I believe in marriage. I have seen love last, between the parents of my friends, and in my own life I have felt the love between Bobby and me grow over a period of four years. I have been touched by the curative powers of love, its comfort, challenge, and constancy.

I am more optimistic than I would have thought possible—perhaps even a little idealistic, which is fine if it doesn't get out of hand. However, my idealism is tempered with a strong layer of realism. I will not enter a marriage with the hardheaded notion that "this *must* work or else," but rather with an awareness of what might lie ahead.

I see that it is a wonderful accomplishment, almost a miracle, to be able to find and to work for a lasting love. Love will take on different guises over the years, expand and shrink, roll in and out like waves. I now believe that lifetime intimacy is a risk worth taking.


The members of my family have all been touched, in some way, by the divorces which have surrounded us. When we hear the statistic "one in every two marriages ends in divorce," I realize that *we* are the human statistic. We share a bit of sadness with children everywhere, for we have all lost something precious. Some have lost much, much more than I.

If it is possible, I want to wipe the slate clean. I hope that my brothers and their wives are happy and that they have large, loving families someday. I hope that my sister and I can look to the future bolstered by what we have seen in the past and make a new beginning for our name.